How to Draw DINOSAURS For Kids

I0480883

This Book Belongs To:

____

DRAWING IS EASY

Drawing with the grid method is one of the best methods to get confident at drawing. You can get great results and have fun because it feels like you are doing a puzzle.

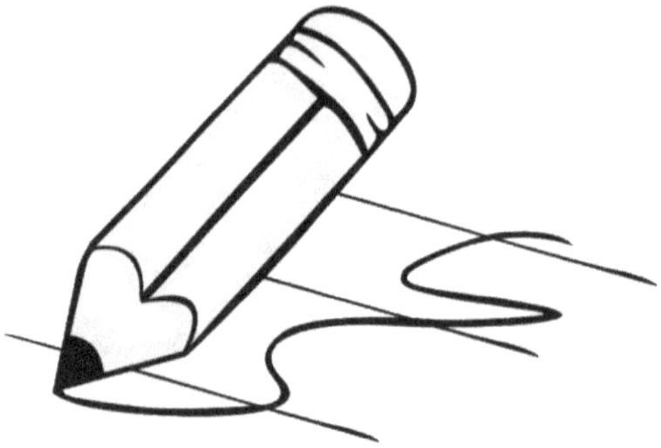

The grid method is used to transfer an image from one sheet of paper to another by using a numbered grid to draw specific squares one at a time to make it easier to draw.

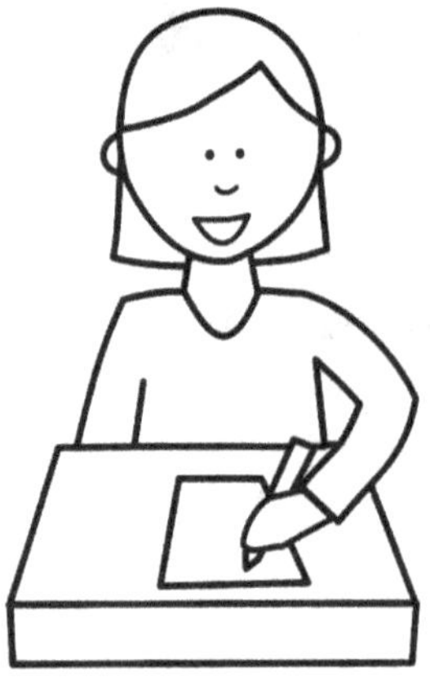

Get ready to learn to draw with this method. You will be able to make identical drawings and with practice you will be able to draw without the grid.

Instructions

Begin by working on one square and copying it the best you can. Start from the top left square and work your way down until you fill them all. You can also draw the outline of the drawing first and then come back to fill in the rest. There is no wrong way of drawing with the grid. Do whatever feels comfortable to you and enjoy!

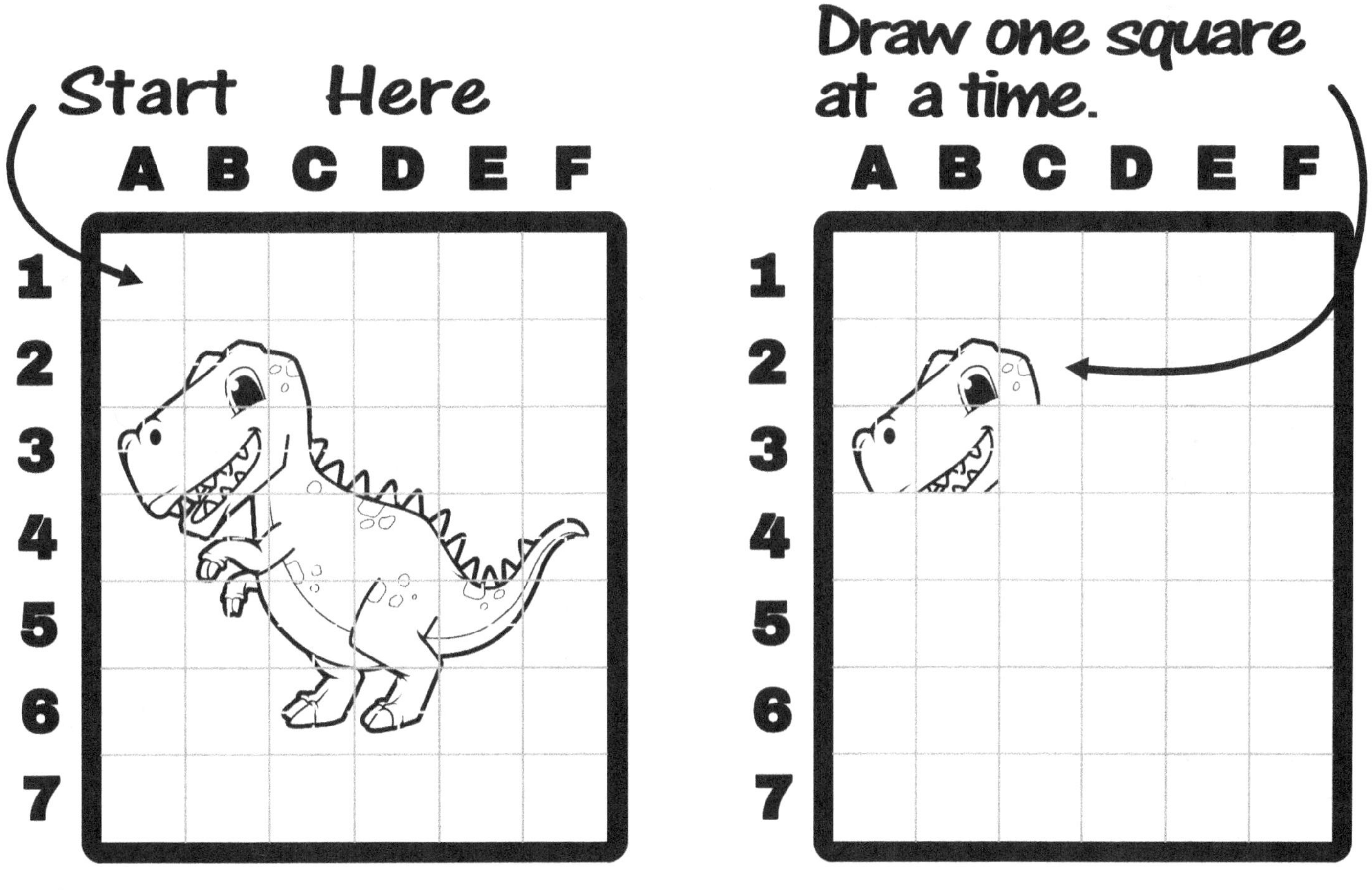

Once you are done drawing, you can color it or continue drawing the rest of the Dinosaurs.

Now Let's Draw!

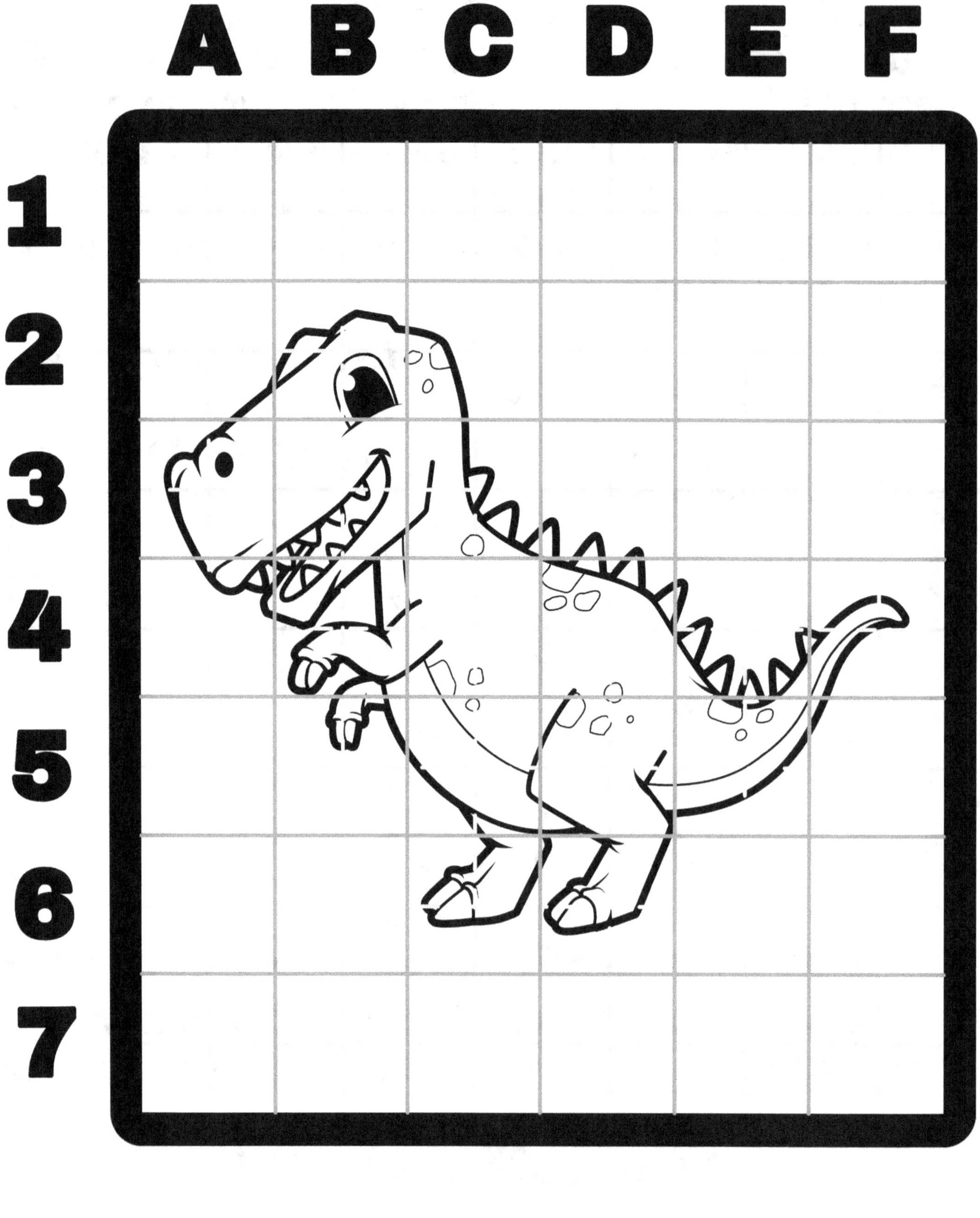
A B C D E F
1
2
3
4
5
6
7

YOUR TURN!

	A	B	C	D	E	F
1						
2						
3						
4						
5						
6						
7						

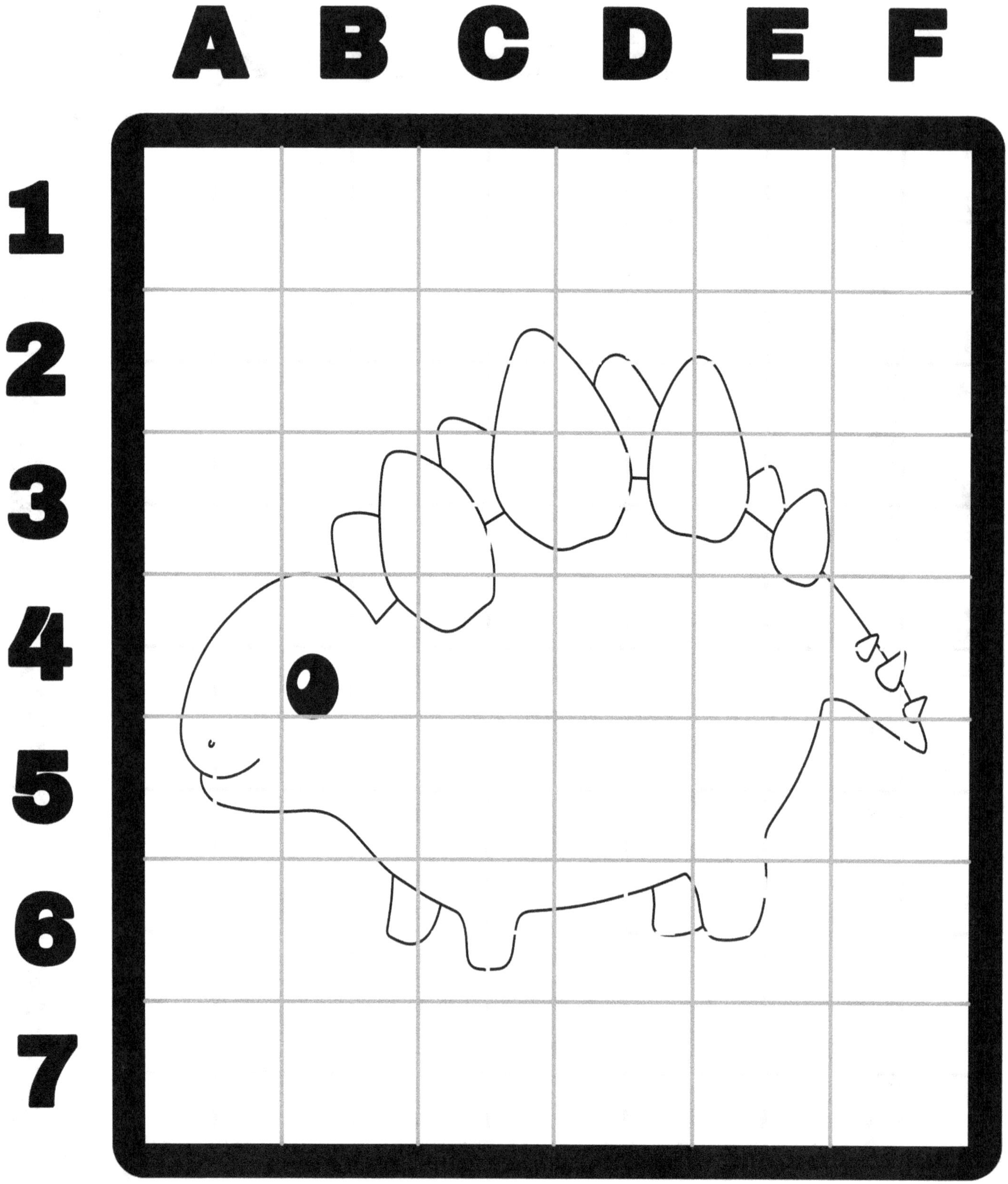
A B C D E F
1
2
3
4
5
6
7

YOUR TURN!

	A	B	C	D	E	F
1						
2						
3						
4						
5						
6						
7						

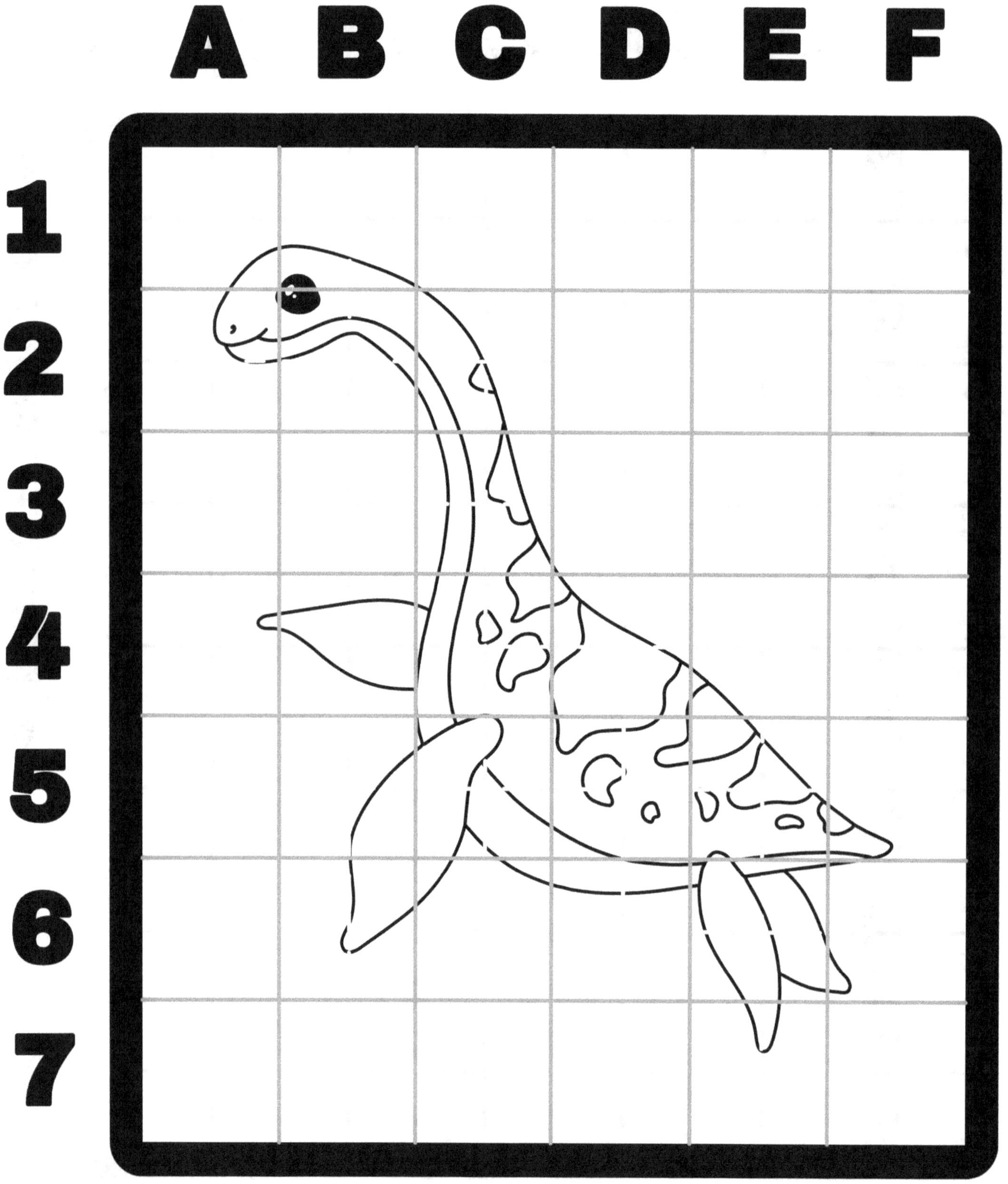
A B C D E F
1
2
3
4
5
6
7

YOUR TURN!

	A	B	C	D	E	F
1						
2						
3						
4						
5						
6						
7						

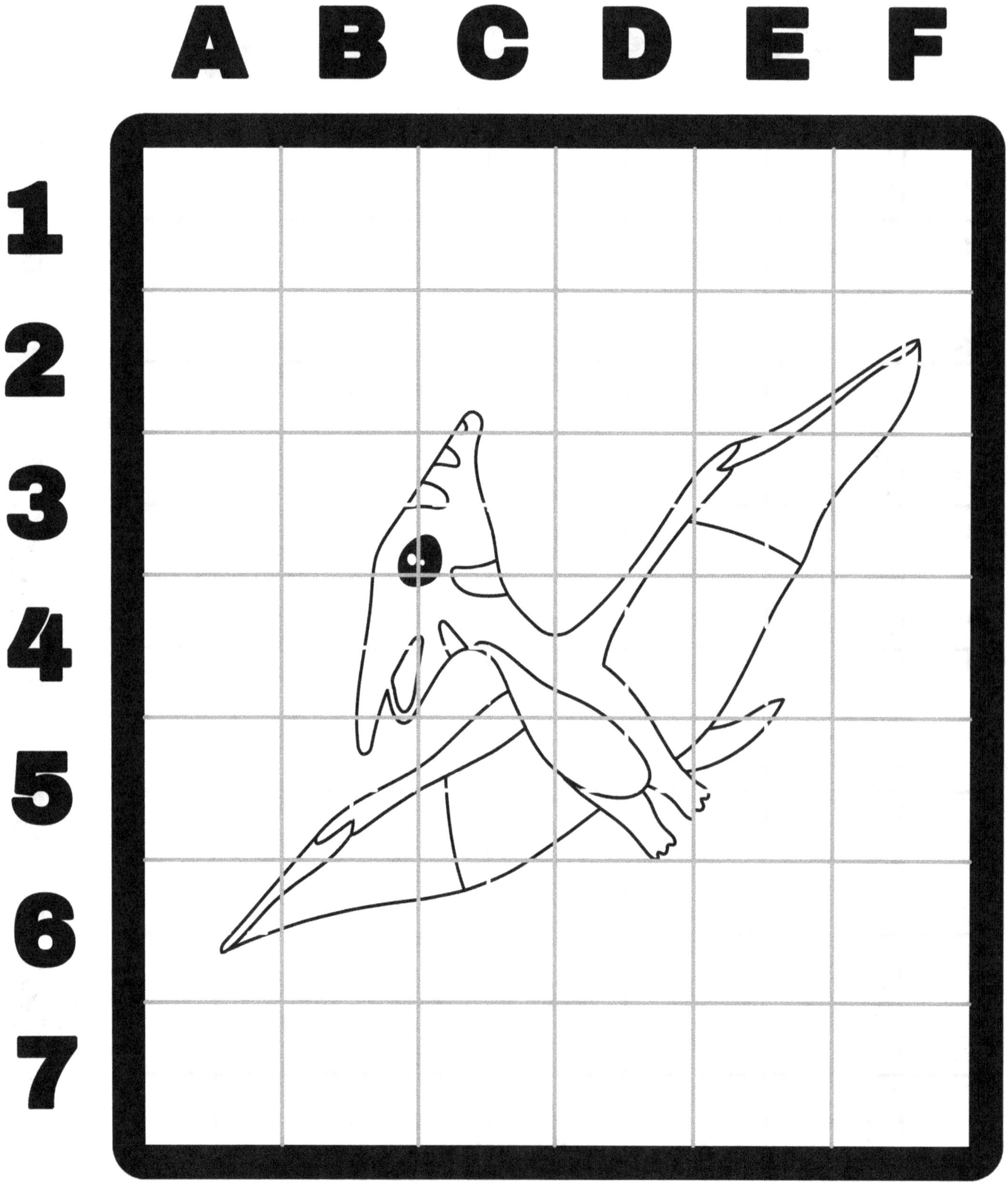
A B C D E F
1
2
3
4
5
6
7

YOUR TURN!

	A	B	C	D	E	F
1						
2						
3						
4						
5						
6						
7						

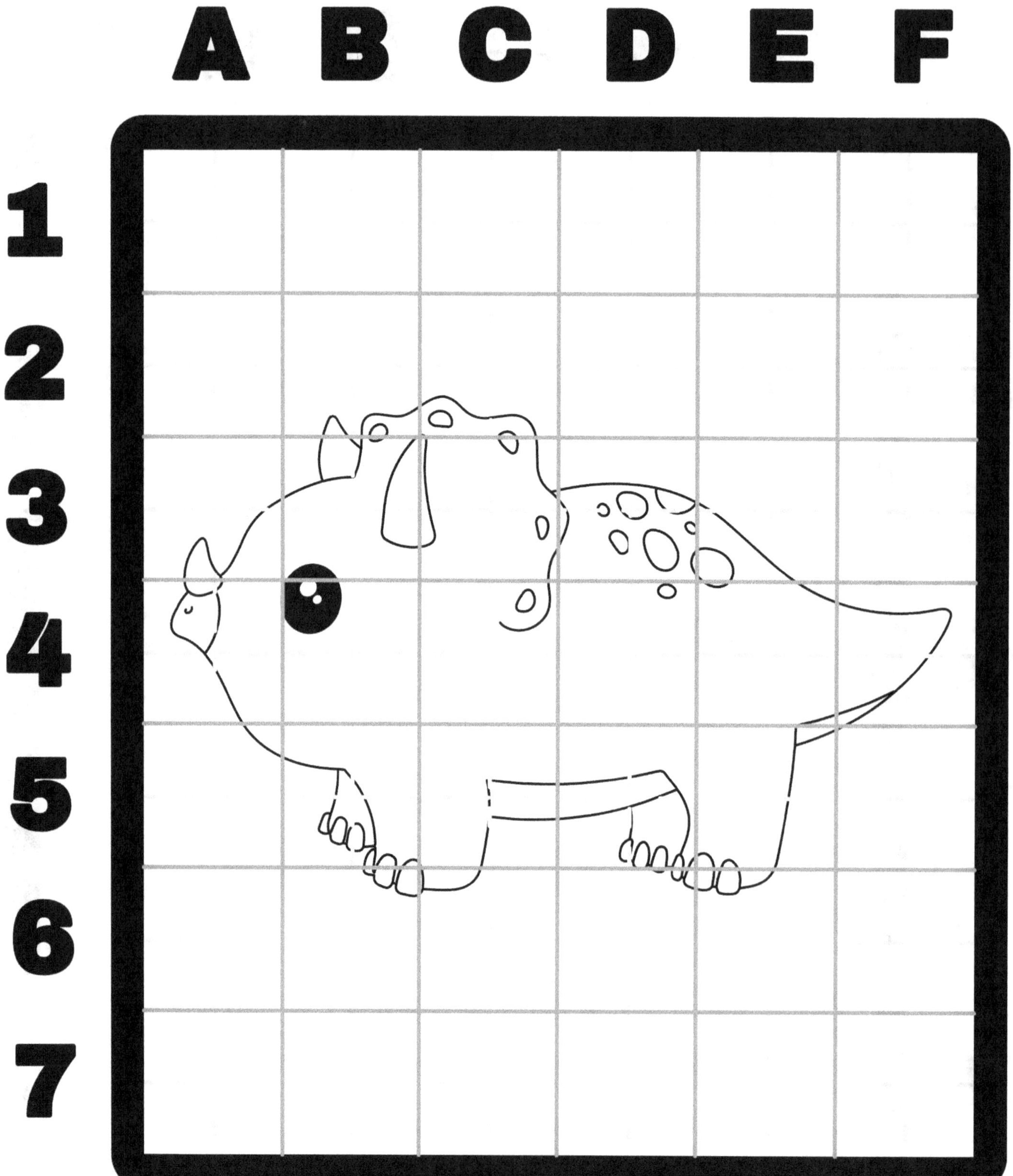
A B C D E F
1
2
3
4
5
6
7

YOUR TURN!

	A	B	C	D	E	F
1						
2						
3						
4						
5						
6						
7						

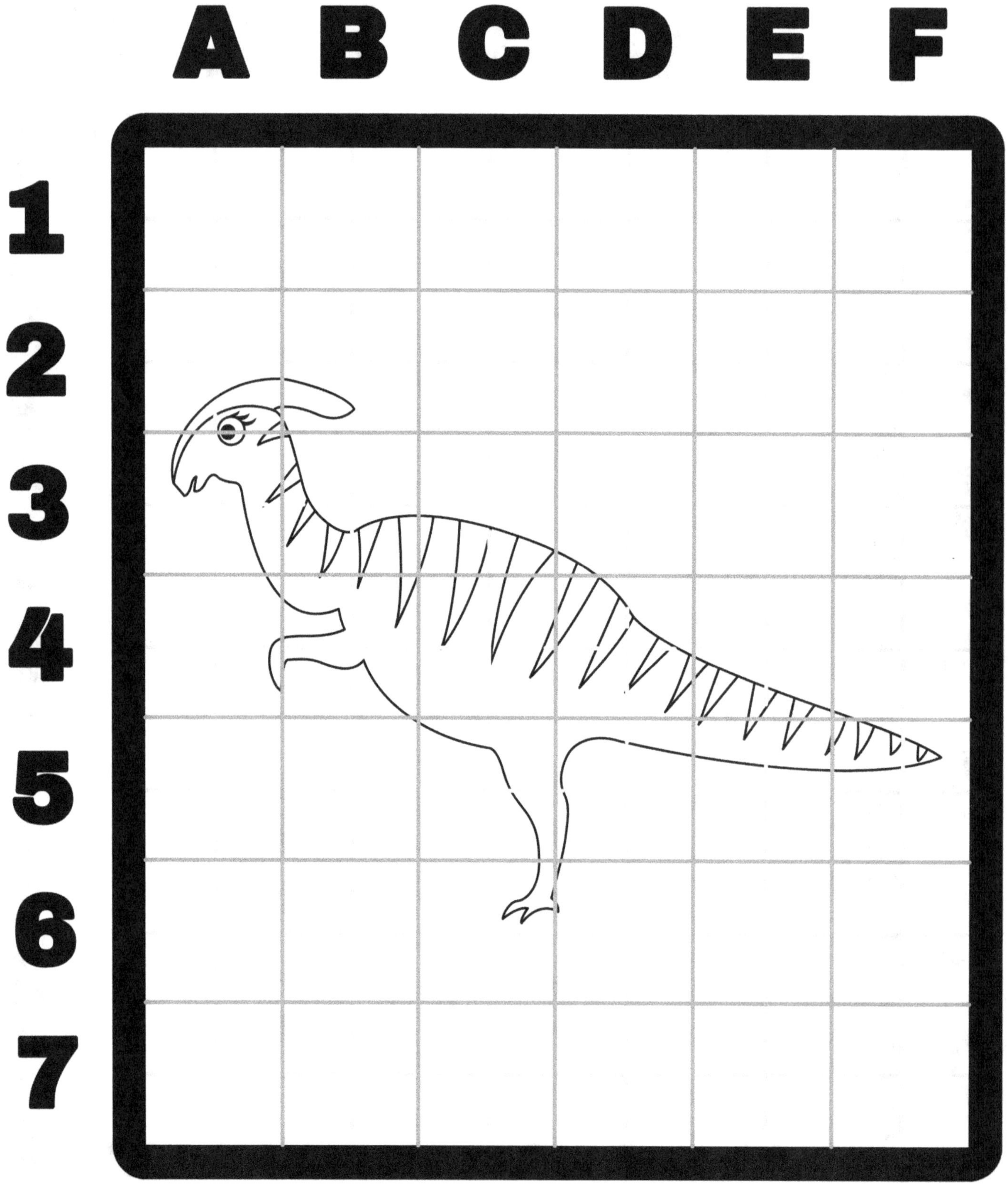
A B C D E F
1
2
3
4
5
6
7

YOUR TURN!

	A	B	C	D	E	F
1						
2						
3						
4						
5						
6						
7						

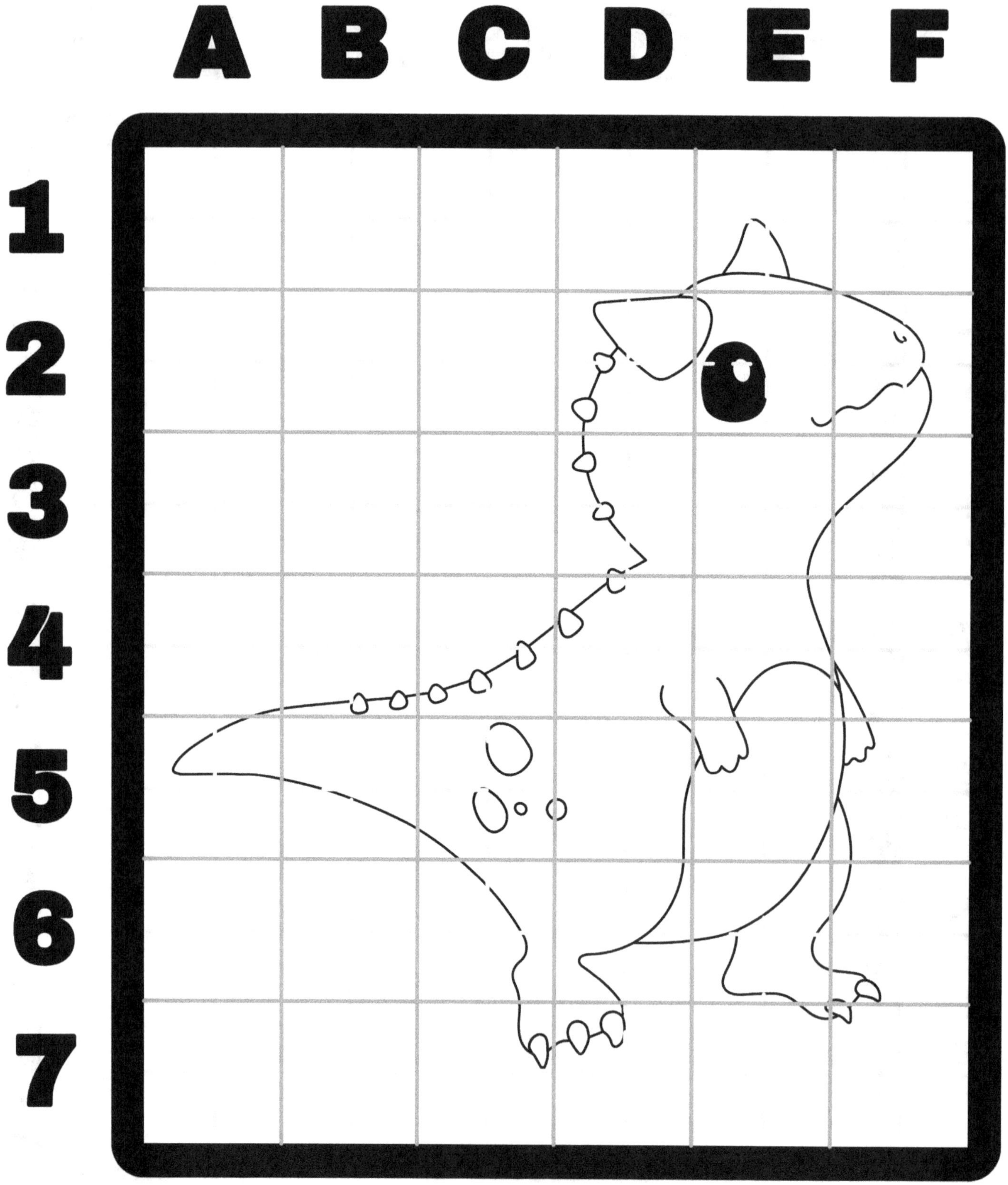
A B C D E F
1
2
3
4
5
6
7

YOUR TURN!

	A	B	C	D	E	F
1						
2						
3						
4						
5						
6						
7						

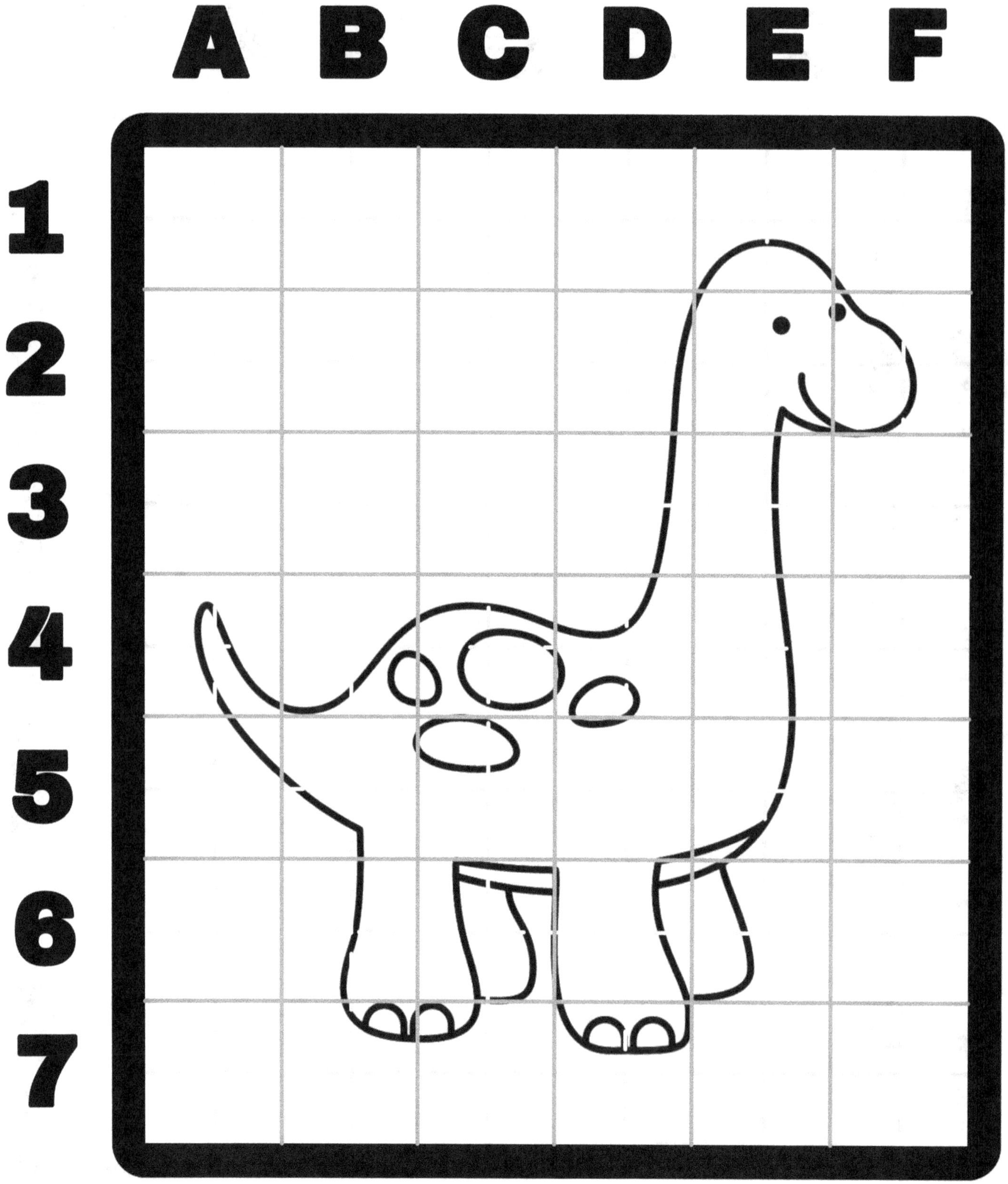
A B C D E F
1
2
3
4
5
6
7

YOUR TURN!

	A	B	C	D	E	F
1						
2						
3						
4						
5						
6						
7						

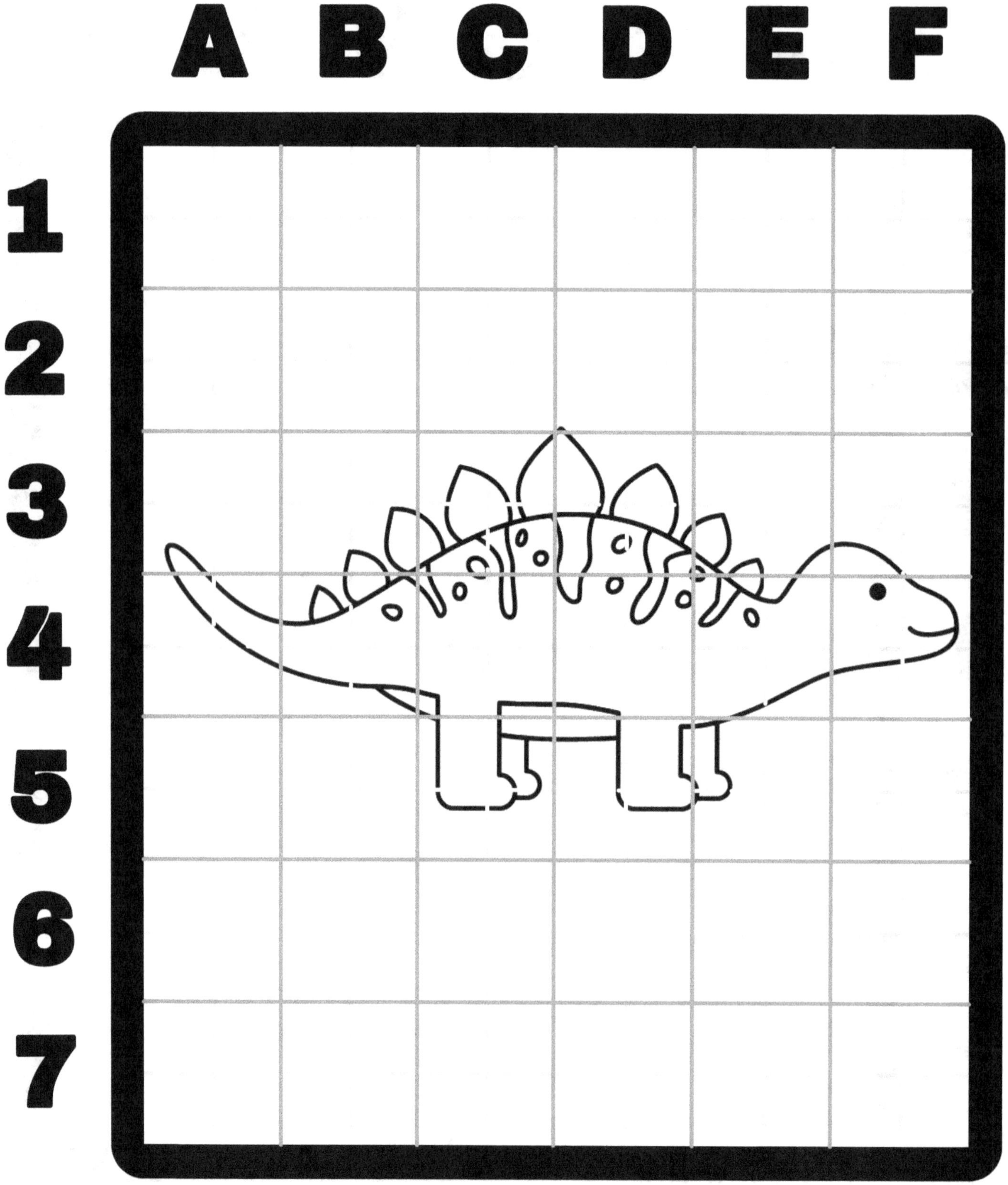
A B C D E F
1
2
3
4
5
6
7

YOUR TURN!

	A	B	C	D	E	F
1						
2						
3						
4						
5						
6						
7						

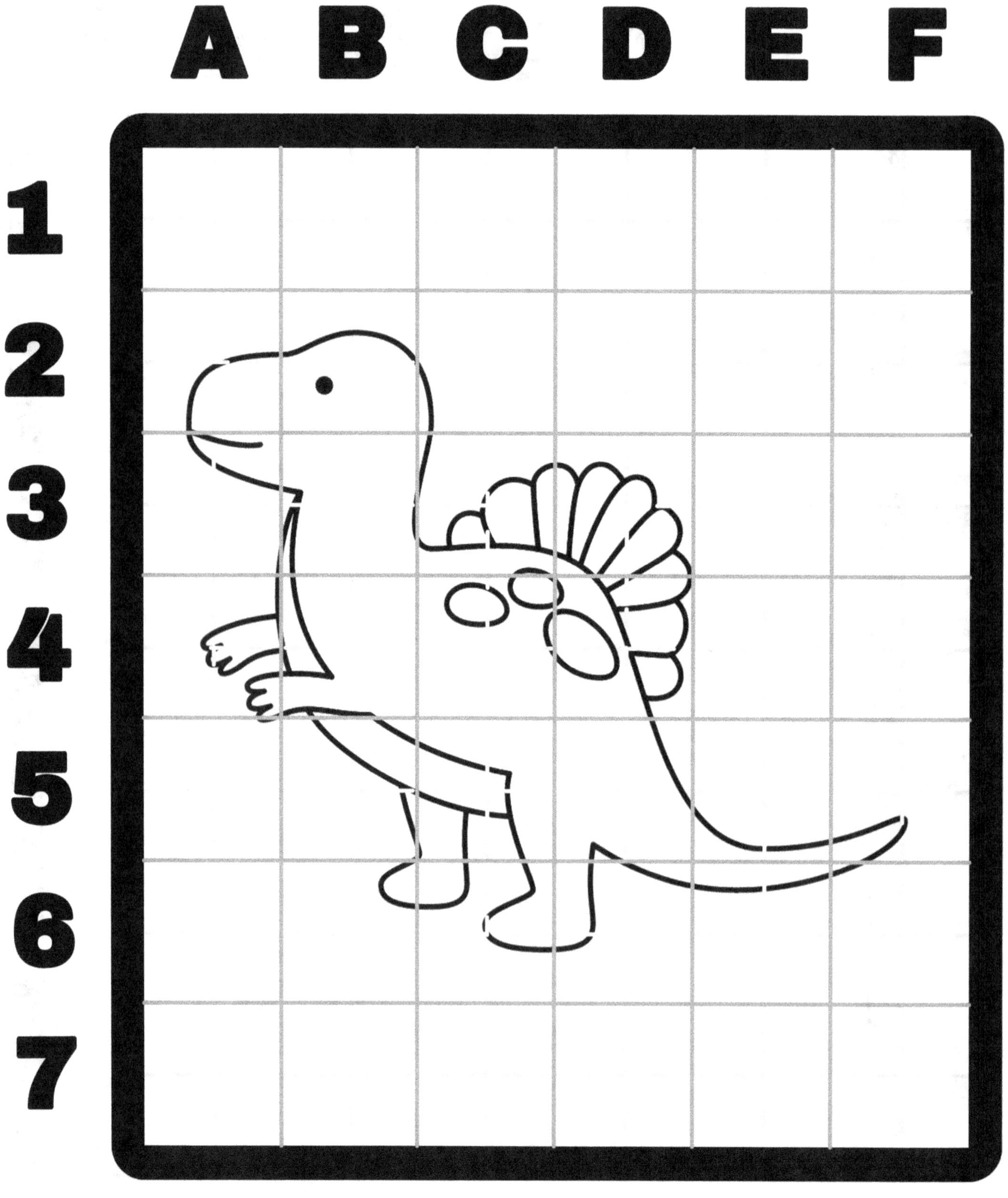
A
B
C
D
E
F
1
2
3
4
5
6
7

YOUR TURN!

	A	B	C	D	E	F
1						
2						
3						
4						
5						
6						
7						

A B C D E F

1 2 3 4 5 6 7

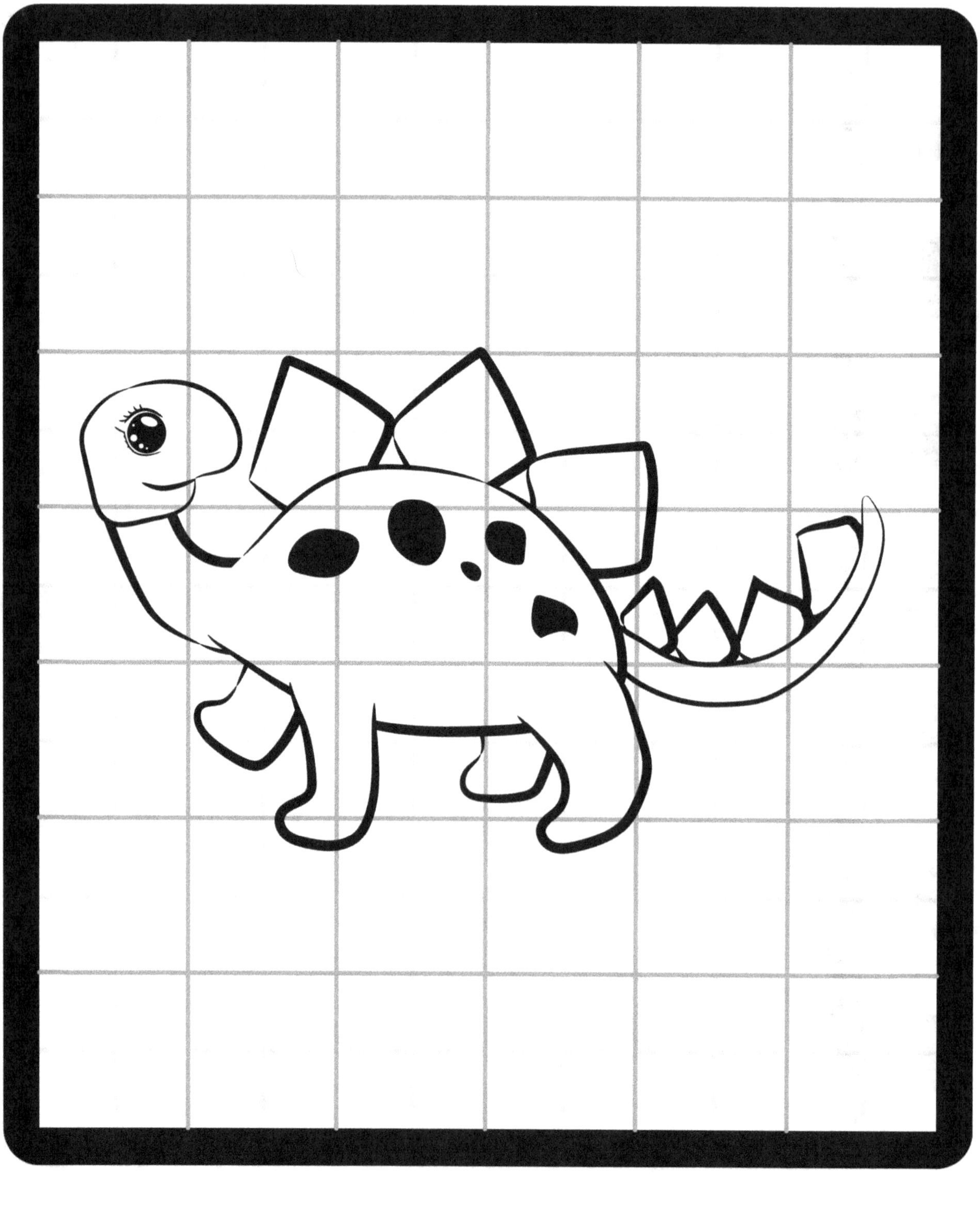

YOUR TURN!

	A	B	C	D	E	F
1						
2						
3						
4						
5						
6						
7						

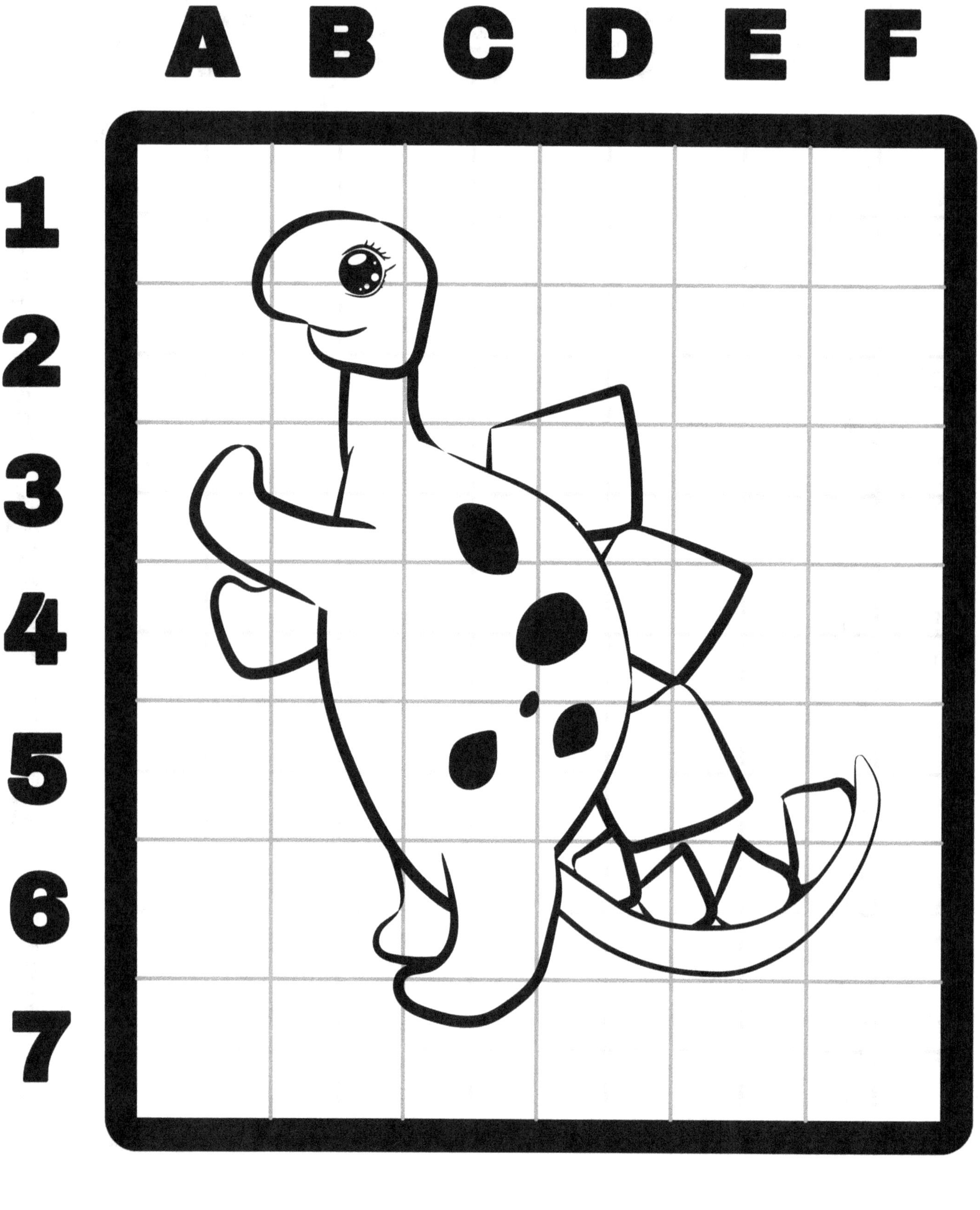
A B C D E F
1
2
3
4
5
6
7

YOUR TURN!

	A	B	C	D	E	F
1						
2						
3						
4						
5						
6						
7						

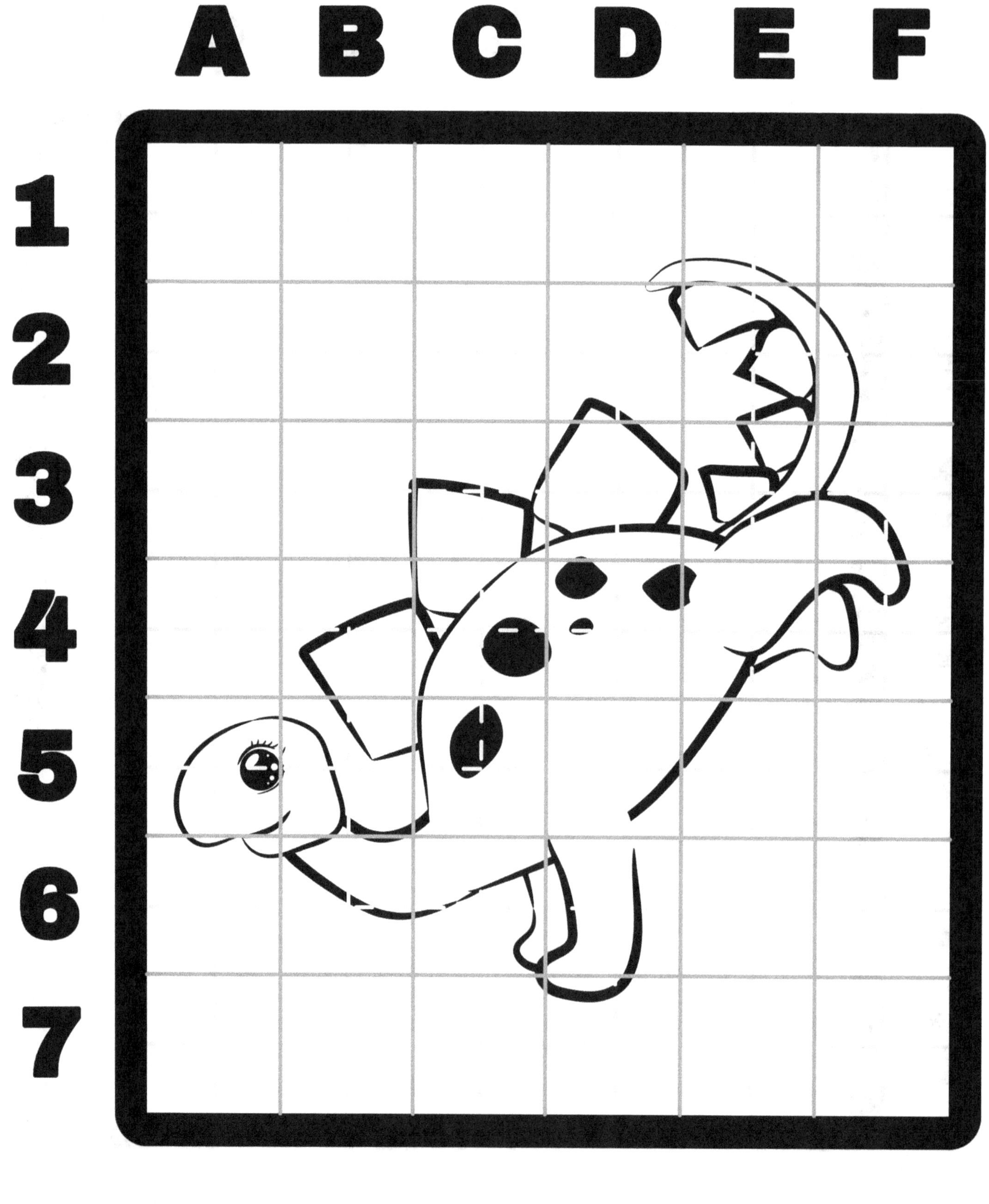
A B C D E F
1
2
3
4
5
6
7

YOUR TURN!

	A	B	C	D	E	F
1						
2						
3						
4						
5						
6						
7						

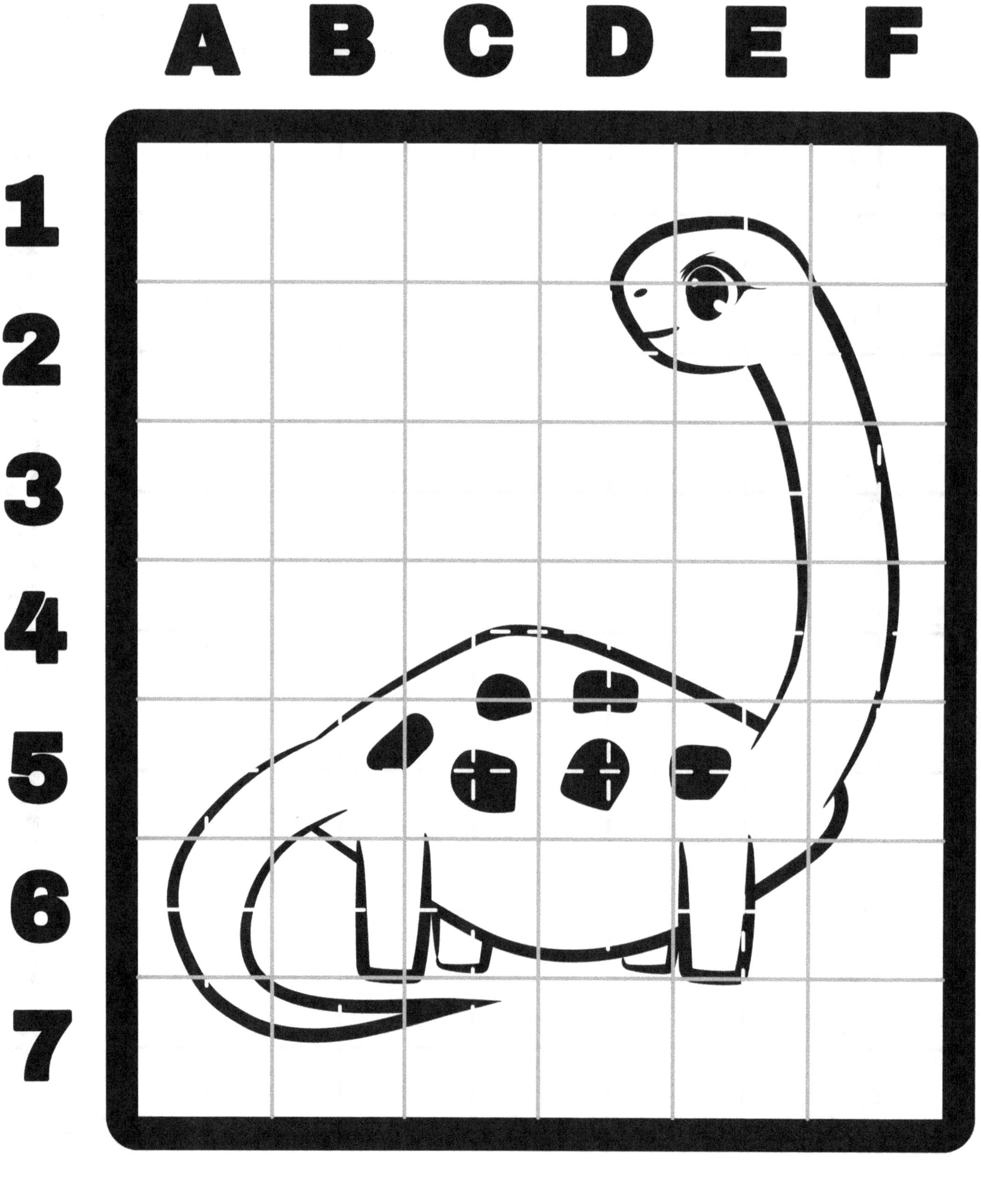
A B C D E F
1
2
3
4
5
6
7

YOUR TURN!

	A	B	C	D	E	F
1						
2						
3						
4						
5						
6						
7						

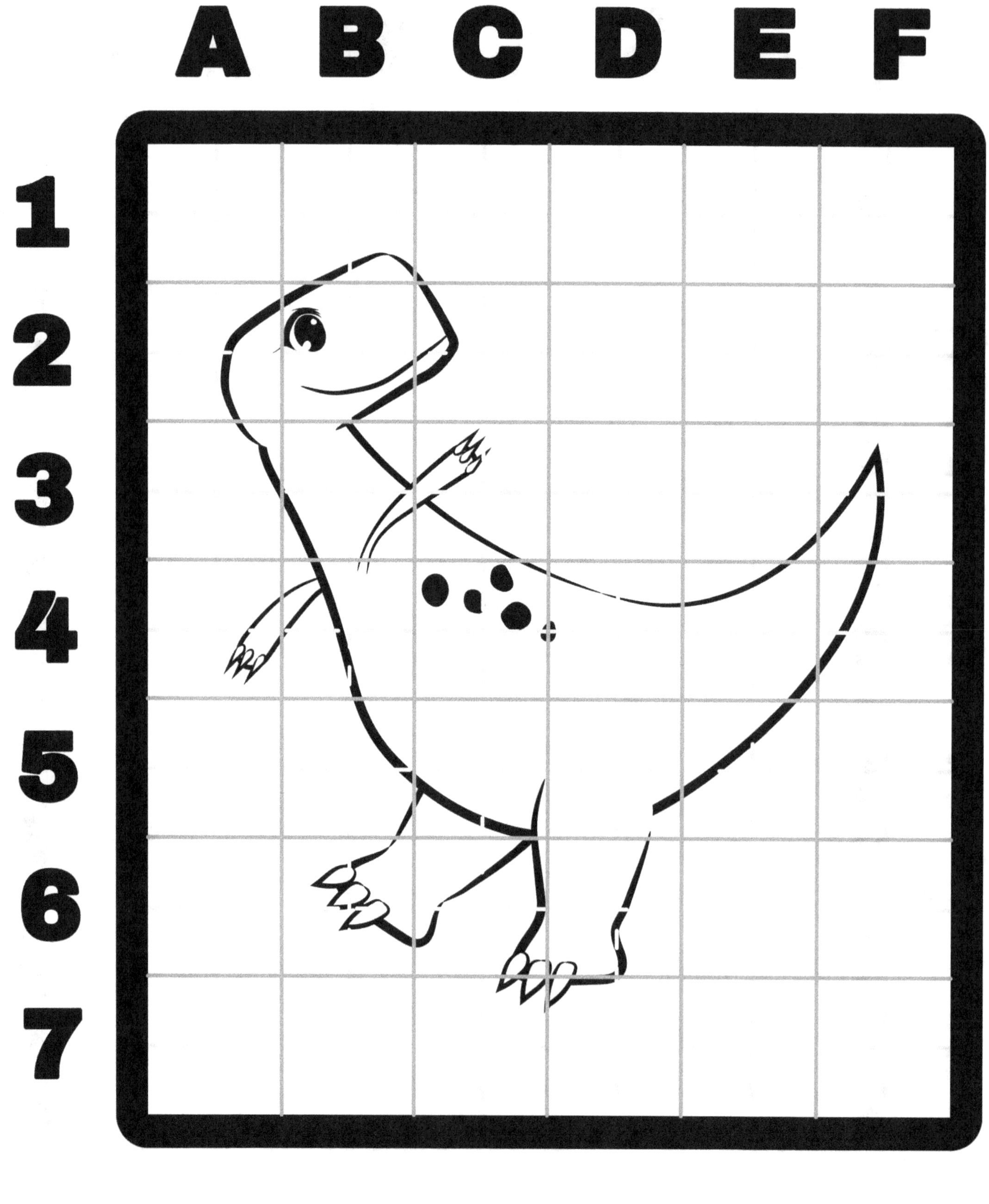
A B C D E F
1
2
3
4
5
6
7

YOUR TURN!

	A	B	C	D	E	F
1						
2						
3						
4						
5						
6						
7						

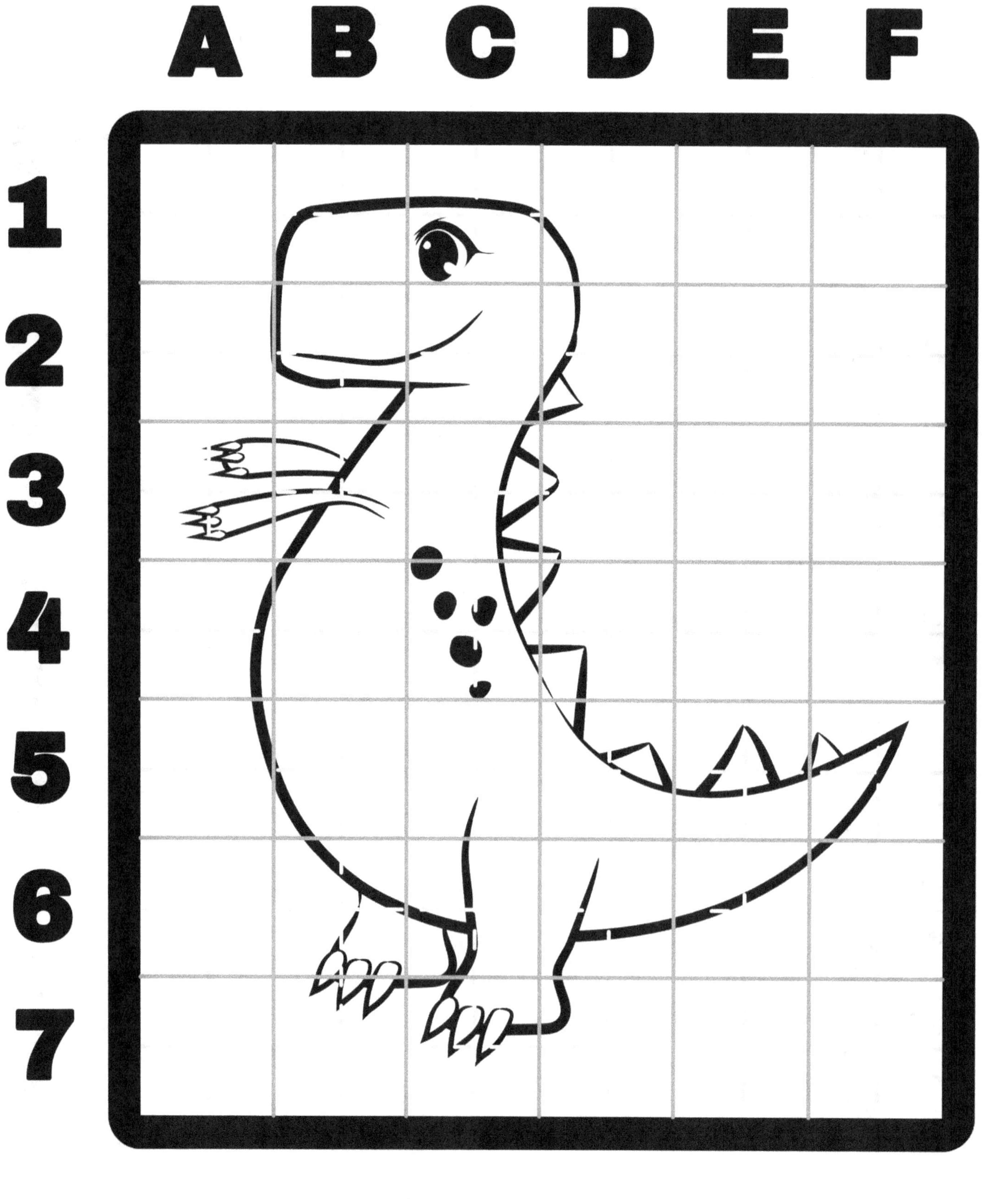
A B C D E F
1
2
3
4
5
6
7

YOUR TURN!

	A	B	C	D	E	F
1						
2						
3						
4						
5						
6						
7						

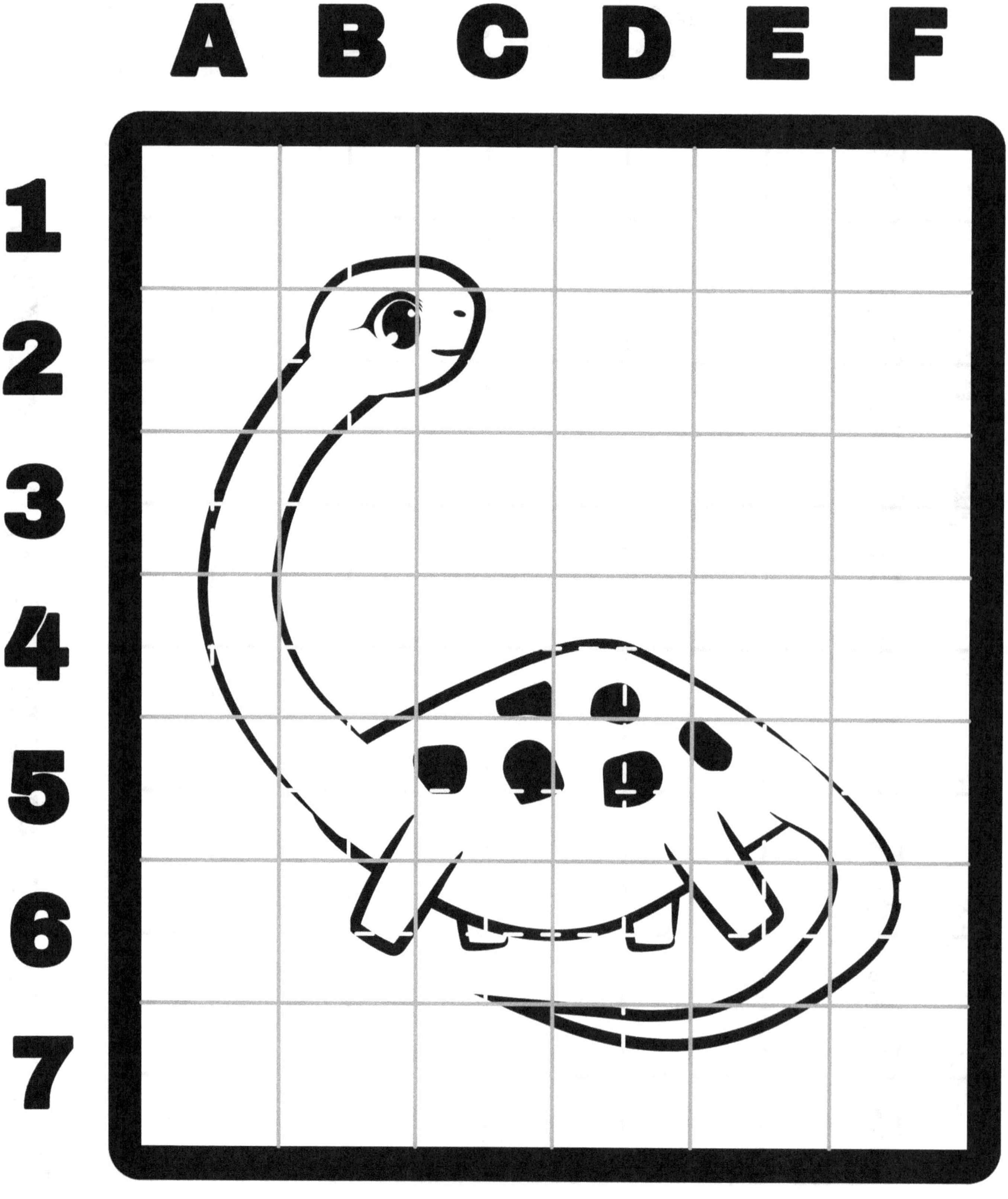
A B C D E F
1
2
3
4
5
6
7

YOUR TURN!

	A	B	C	D	E	F
1						
2						
3						
4						
5						
6						
7						

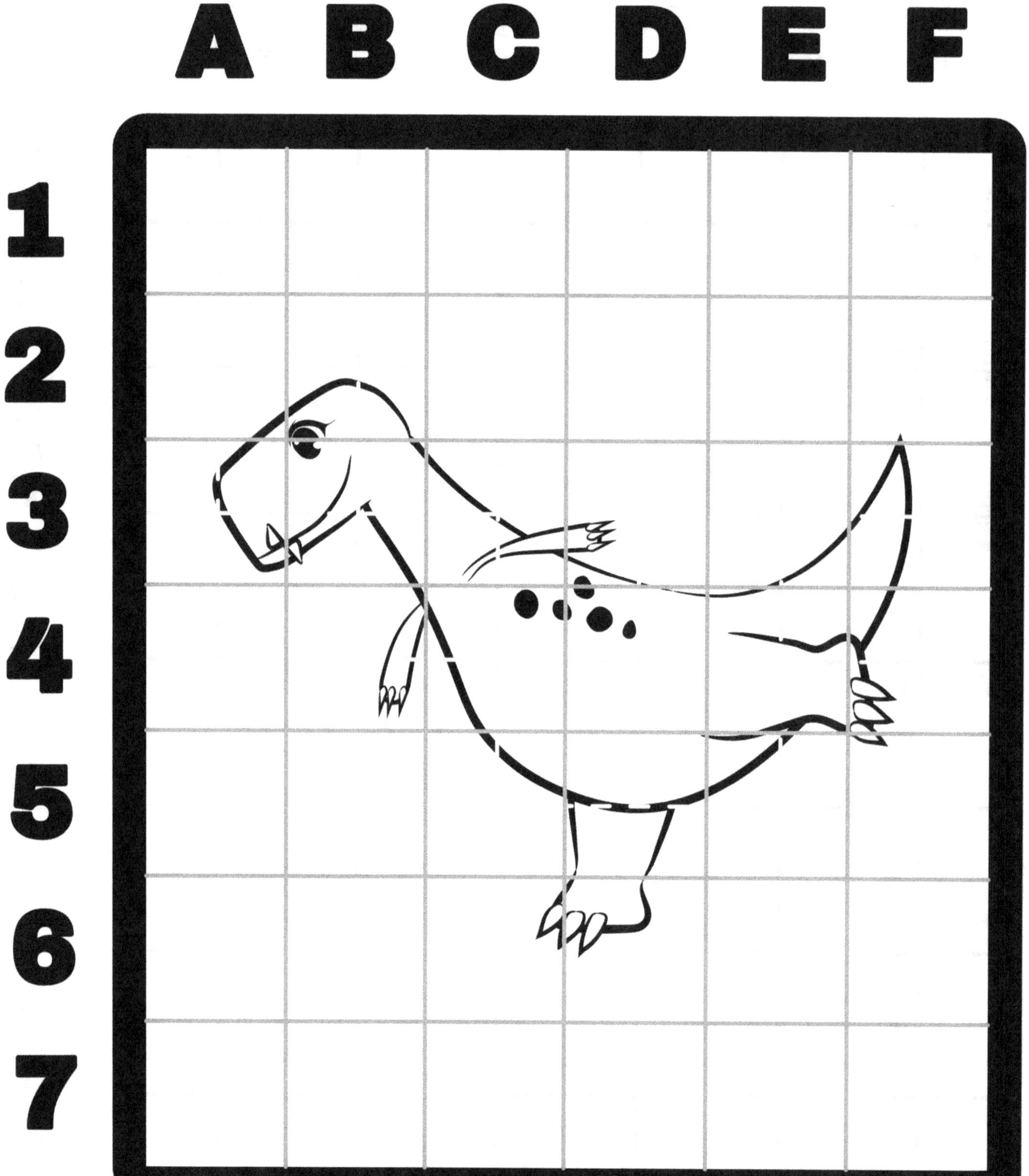
A B C D E F
1
2
3
4
5
6
7

YOUR TURN!

	A	B	C	D	E	F
1						
2						
3						
4						
5						
6						
7						

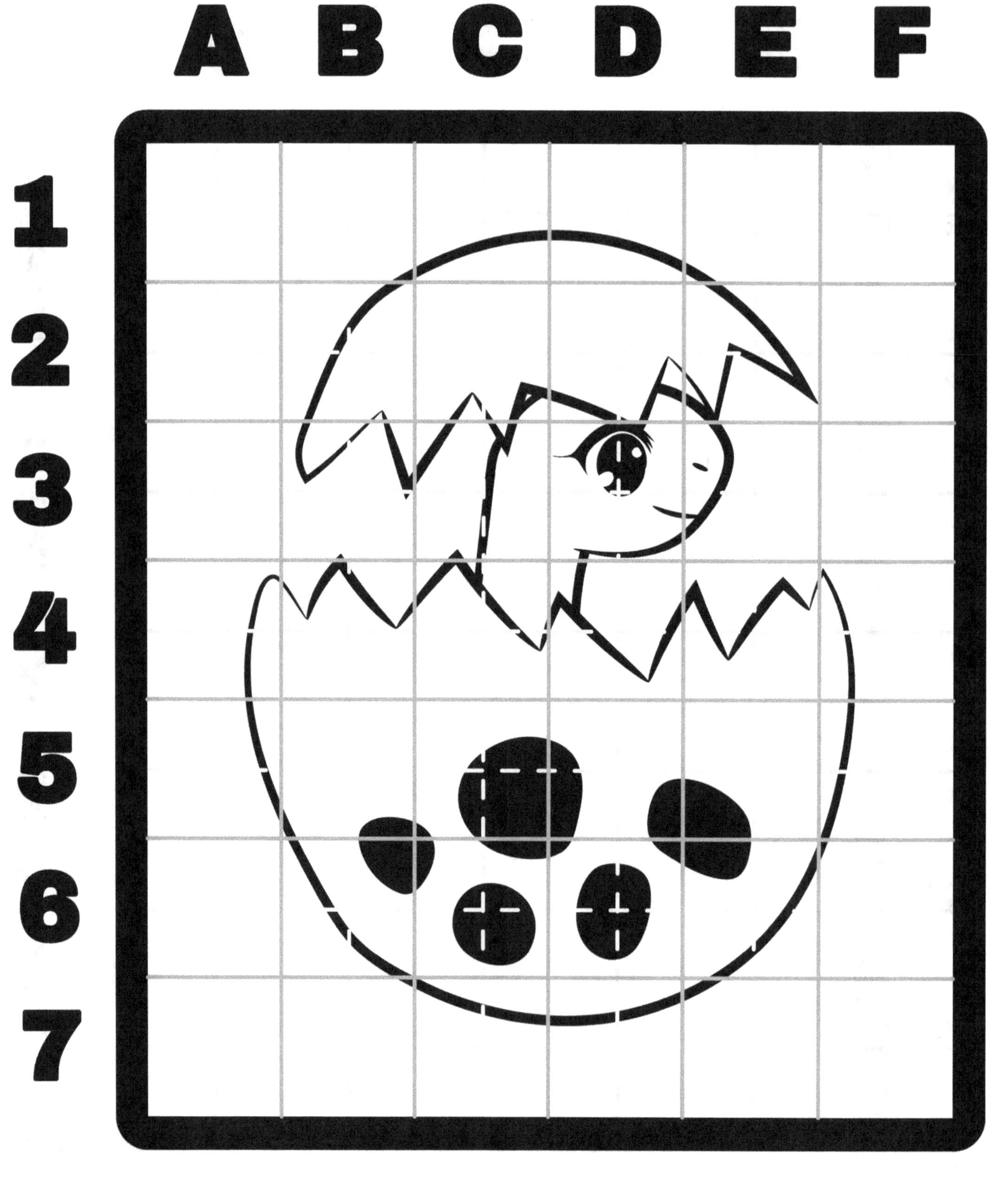
A B C D E F
1
2
3
4
5
6
7

YOUR TURN!

	A	B	C	D	E	F
1						
2						
3						
4						
5						
6						
7						

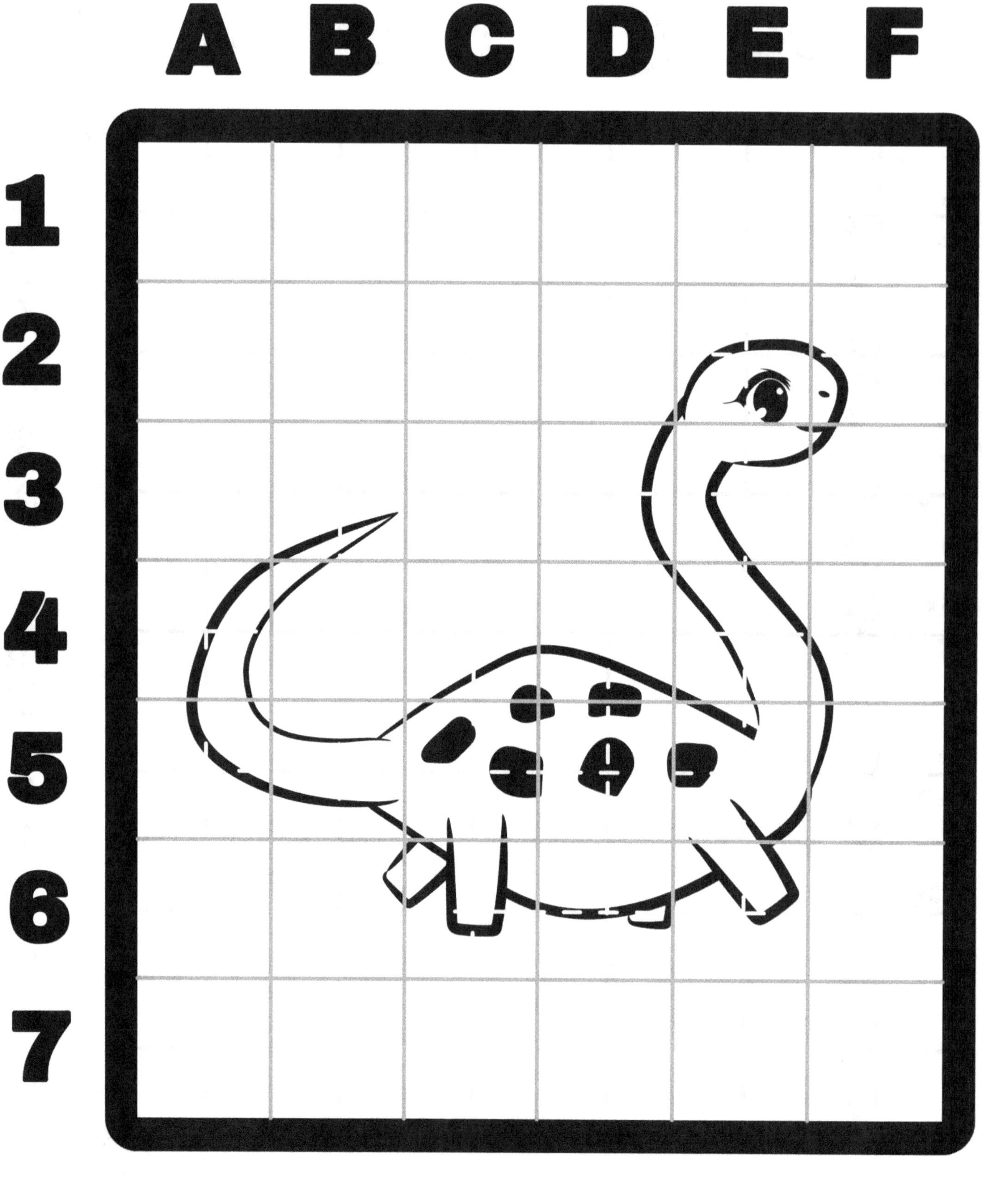
A B C D E F
1
2
3
4
5
6
7

YOUR TURN!

	A	B	C	D	E	F
1						
2						
3						
4						
5						
6						
7						

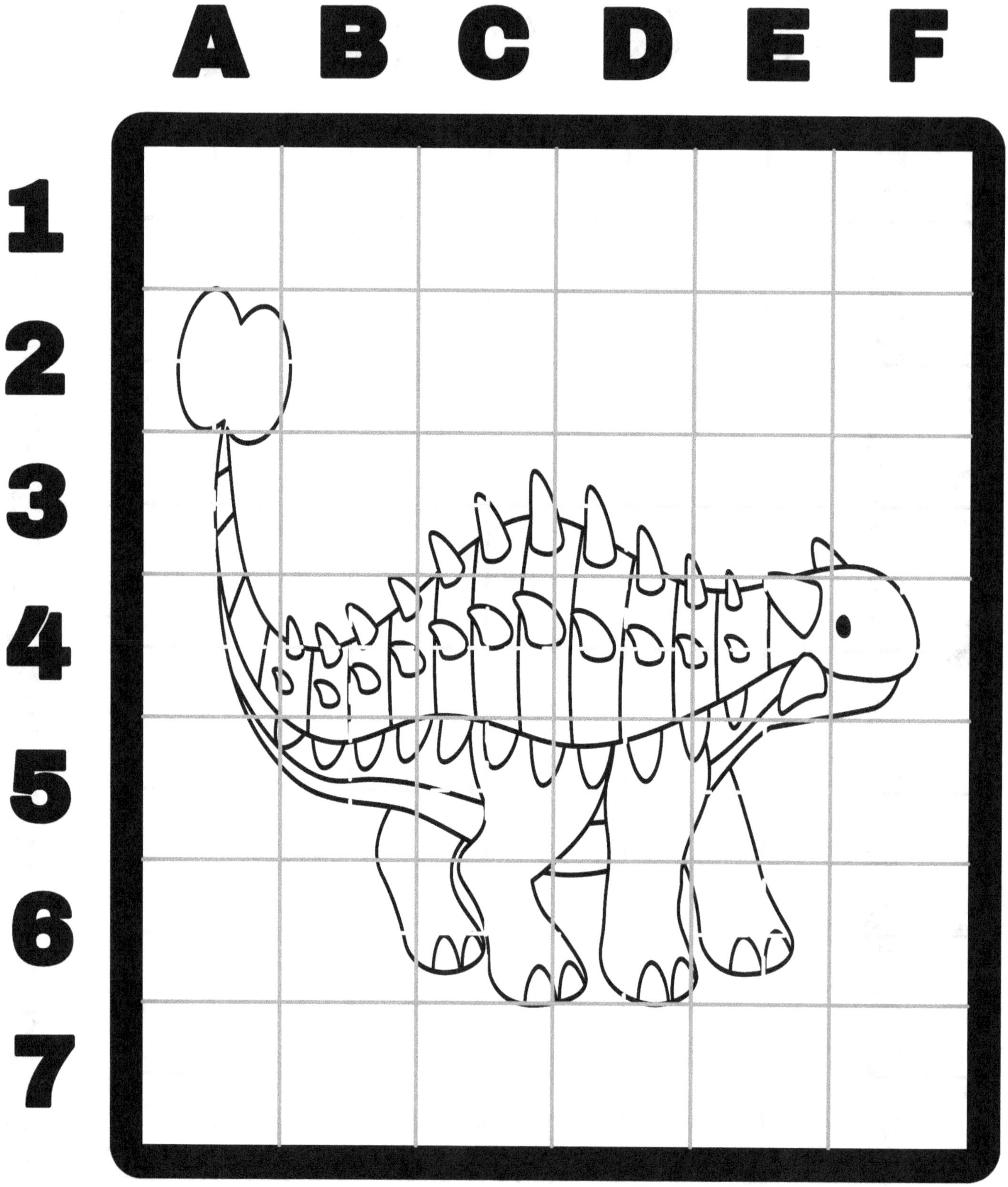
A B C D E F
1
2
3
4
5
6
7

YOUR TURN!

	A	B	C	D	E	F
1						
2						
3						
4						
5						
6						
7						

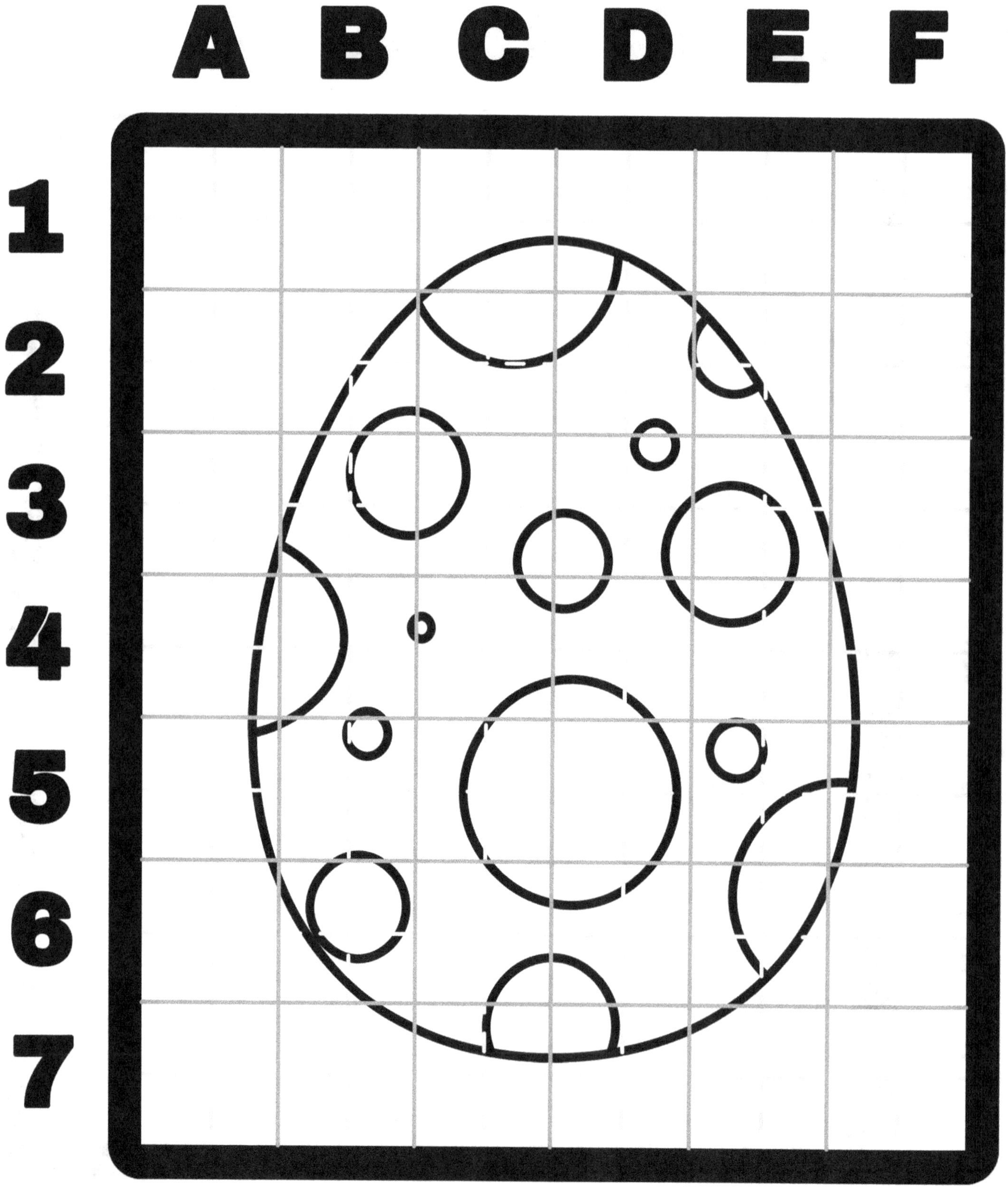
A B C D E F
1
2
3
4
5
6
7

YOUR TURN!

	A	B	C	D	E	F
1						
2						
3						
4						
5						
6						
7						

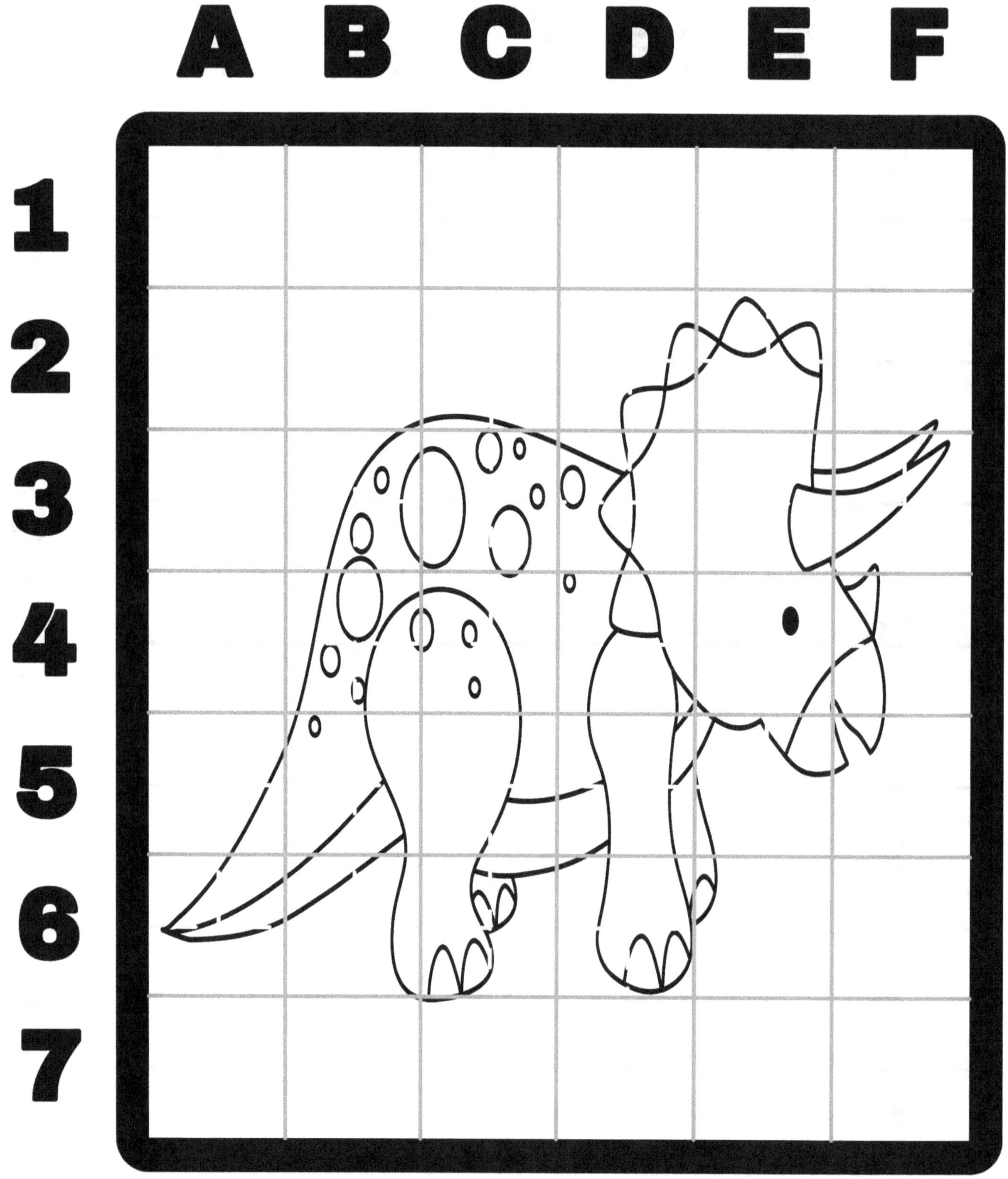
A B C D E F
1
2
3
4
5
6
7

YOUR TURN!

	A	B	C	D	E	F
1						
2						
3						
4						
5						
6						
7						

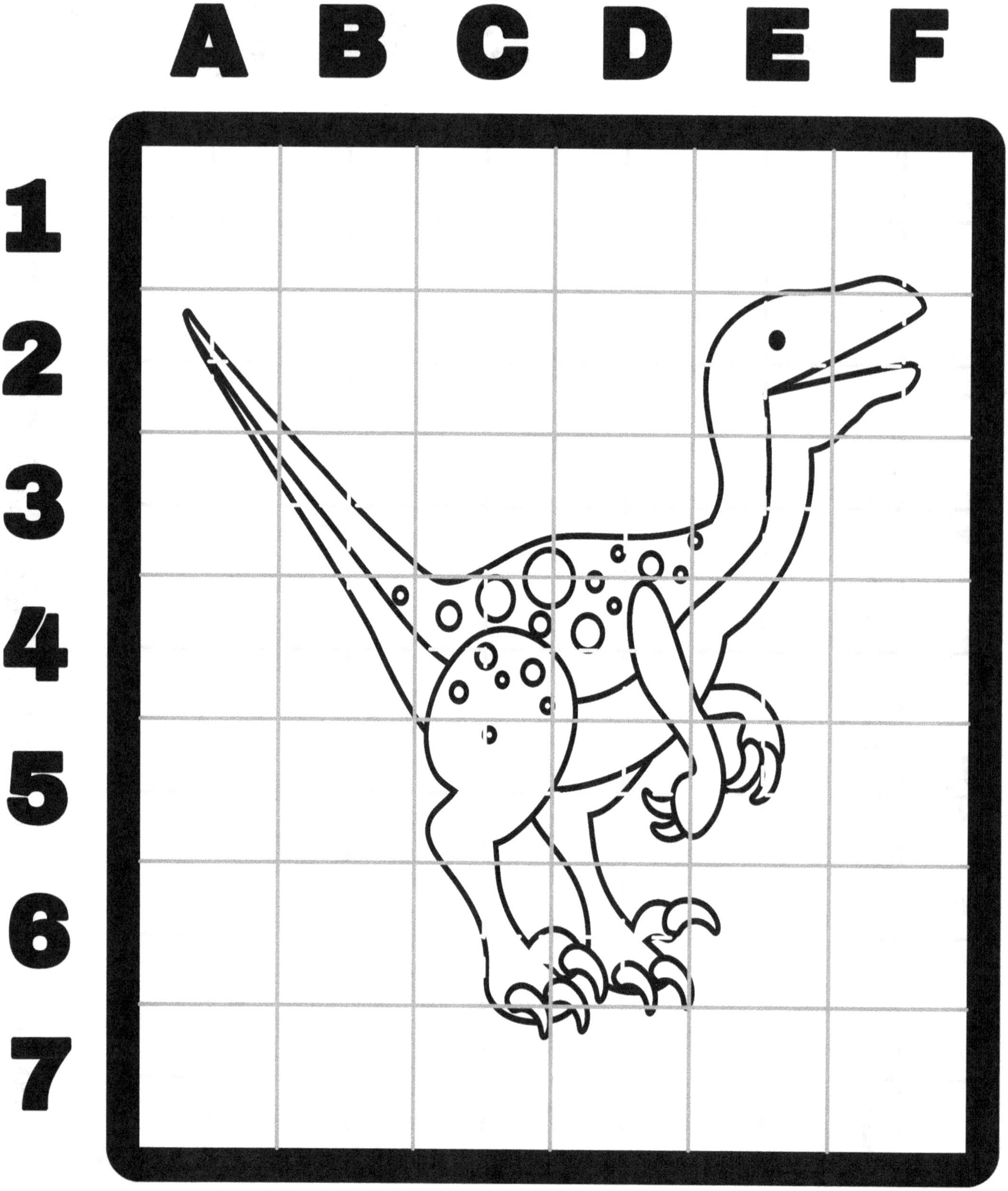
A B C D E F
1
2
3
4
5
6
7

YOUR TURN!

	A	B	C	D	E	F
1						
2						
3						
4						
5						
6						
7						

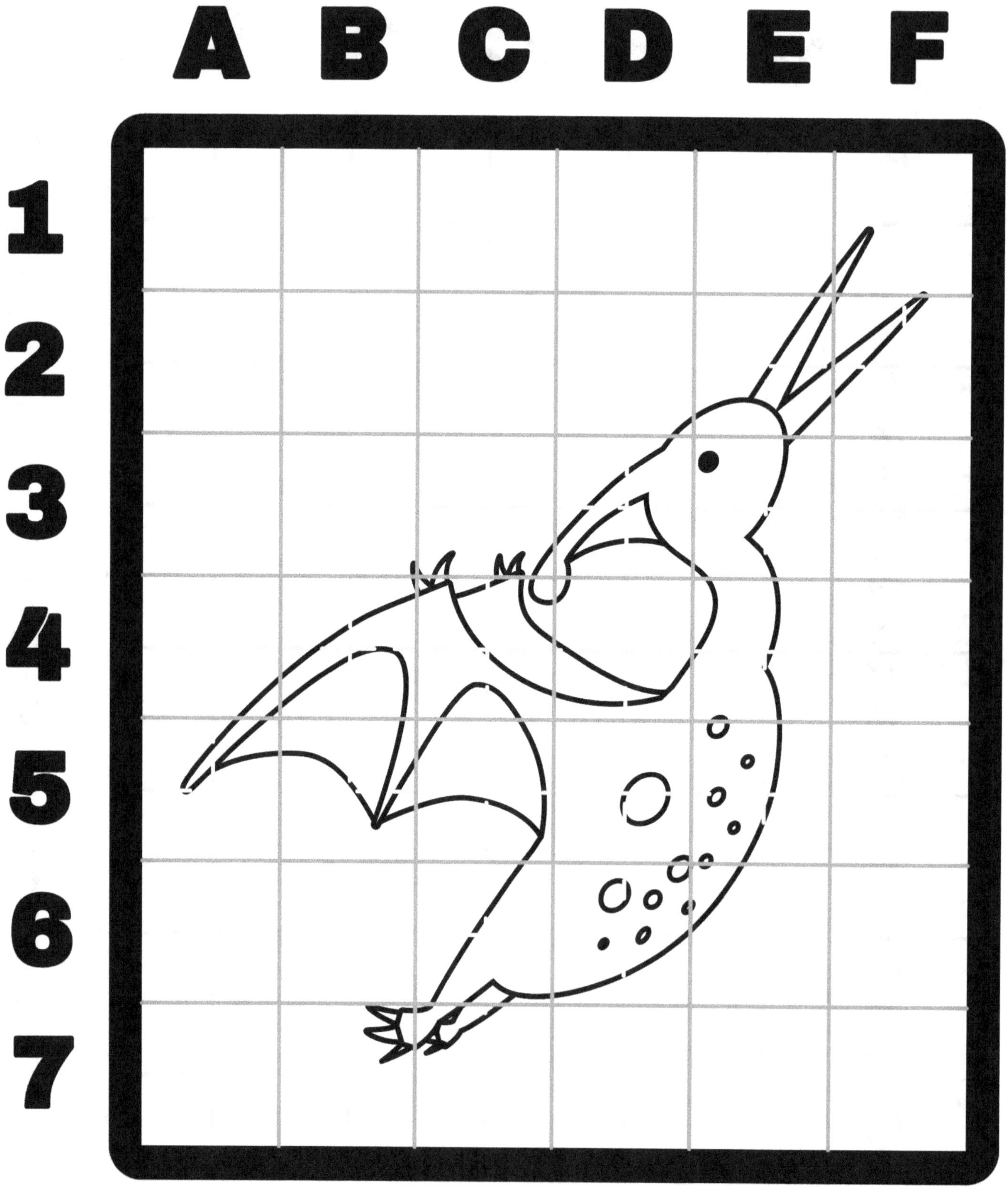
A B C D E F
1
2
3
4
5
6
7

YOUR TURN!

	A	B	C	D	E	F
1						
2						
3						
4						
5						
6						
7						

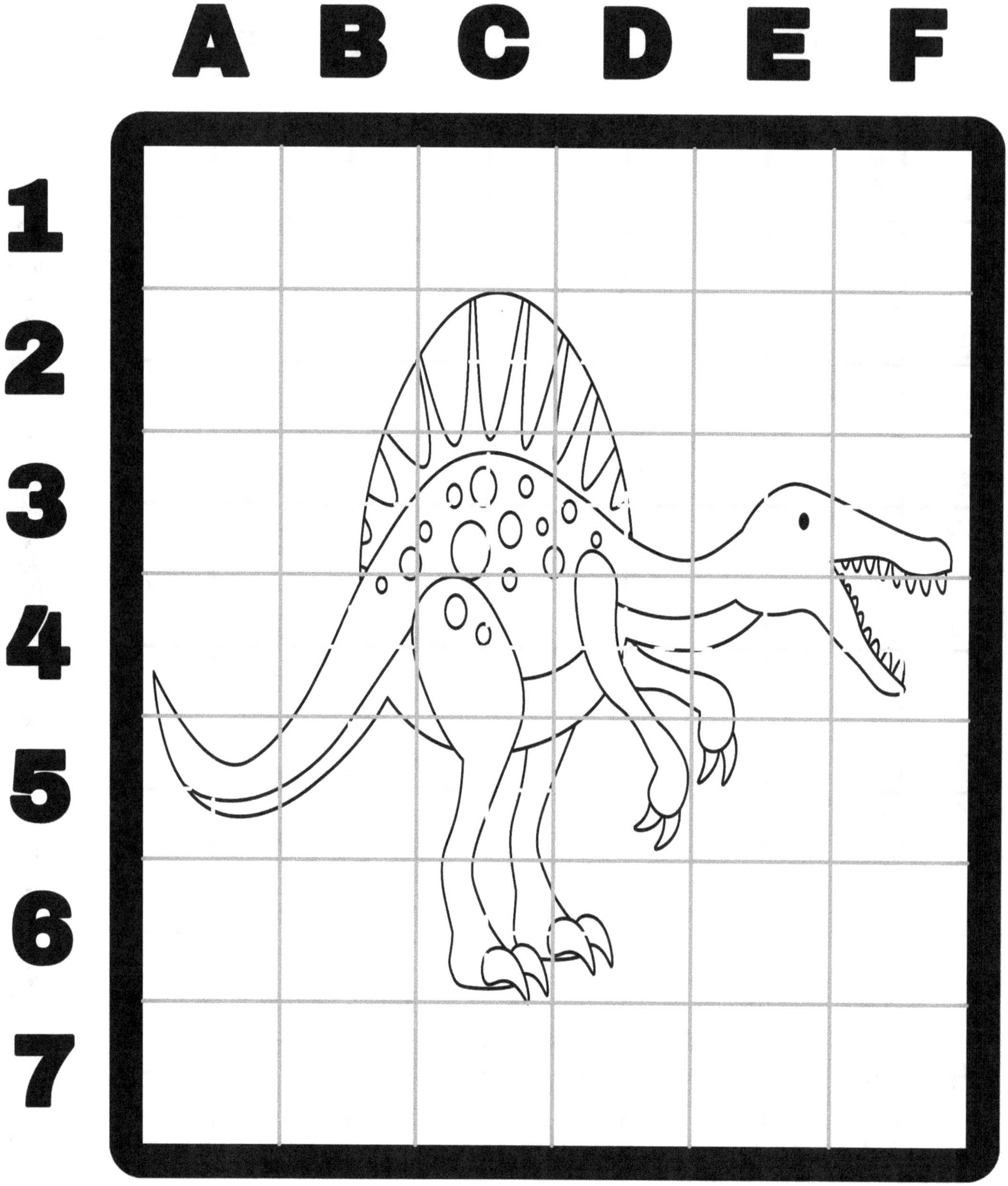
A B C D E F
1
2
3
4
5
6
7

YOUR TURN!

	A	B	C	D	E	F
1						
2						
3						
4						
5						
6						
7						

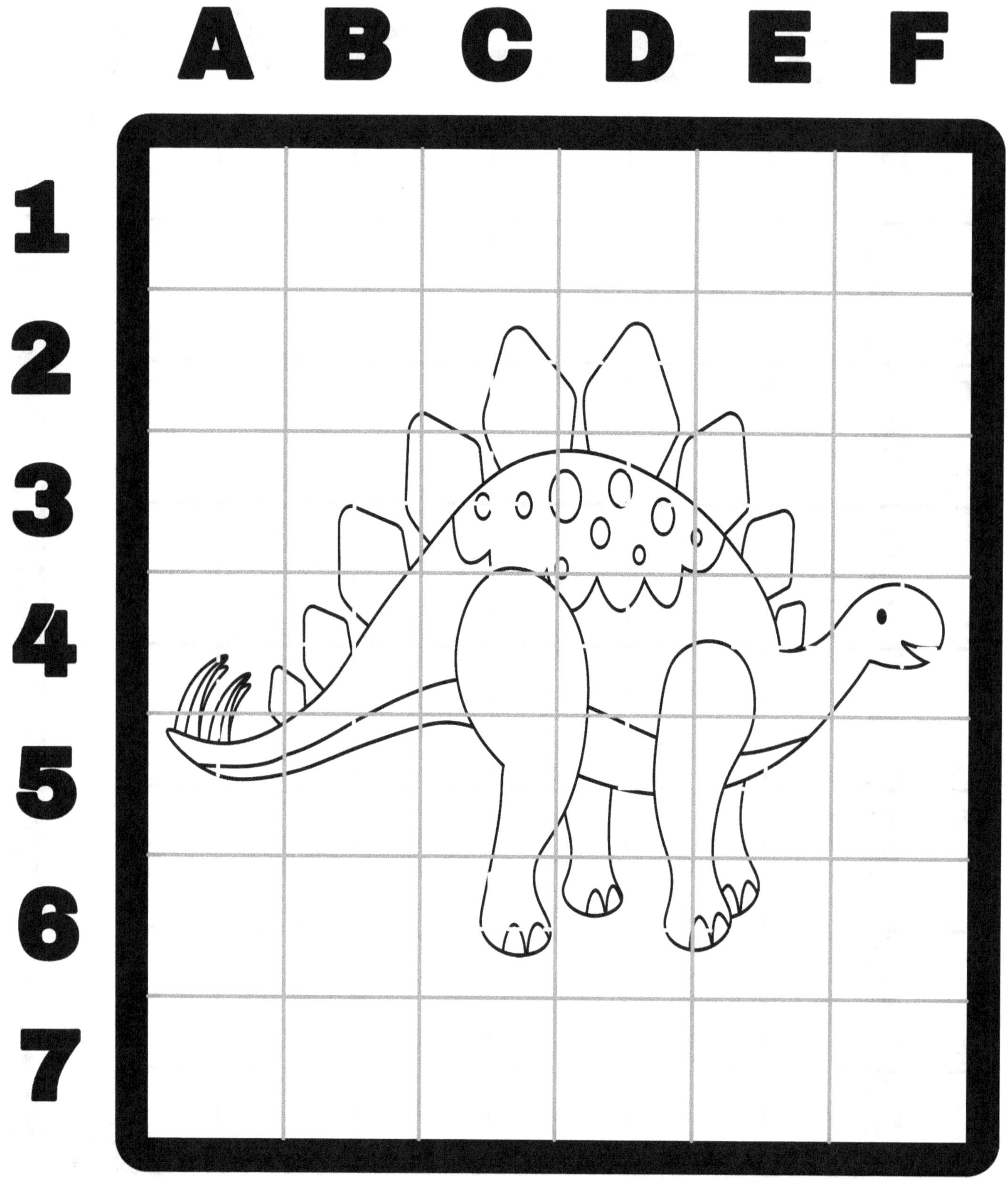
A B C D E F
1
2
3
4
5
6
7

YOUR TURN!

	A	B	C	D	E	F
1						
2						
3						
4						
5						
6						
7						

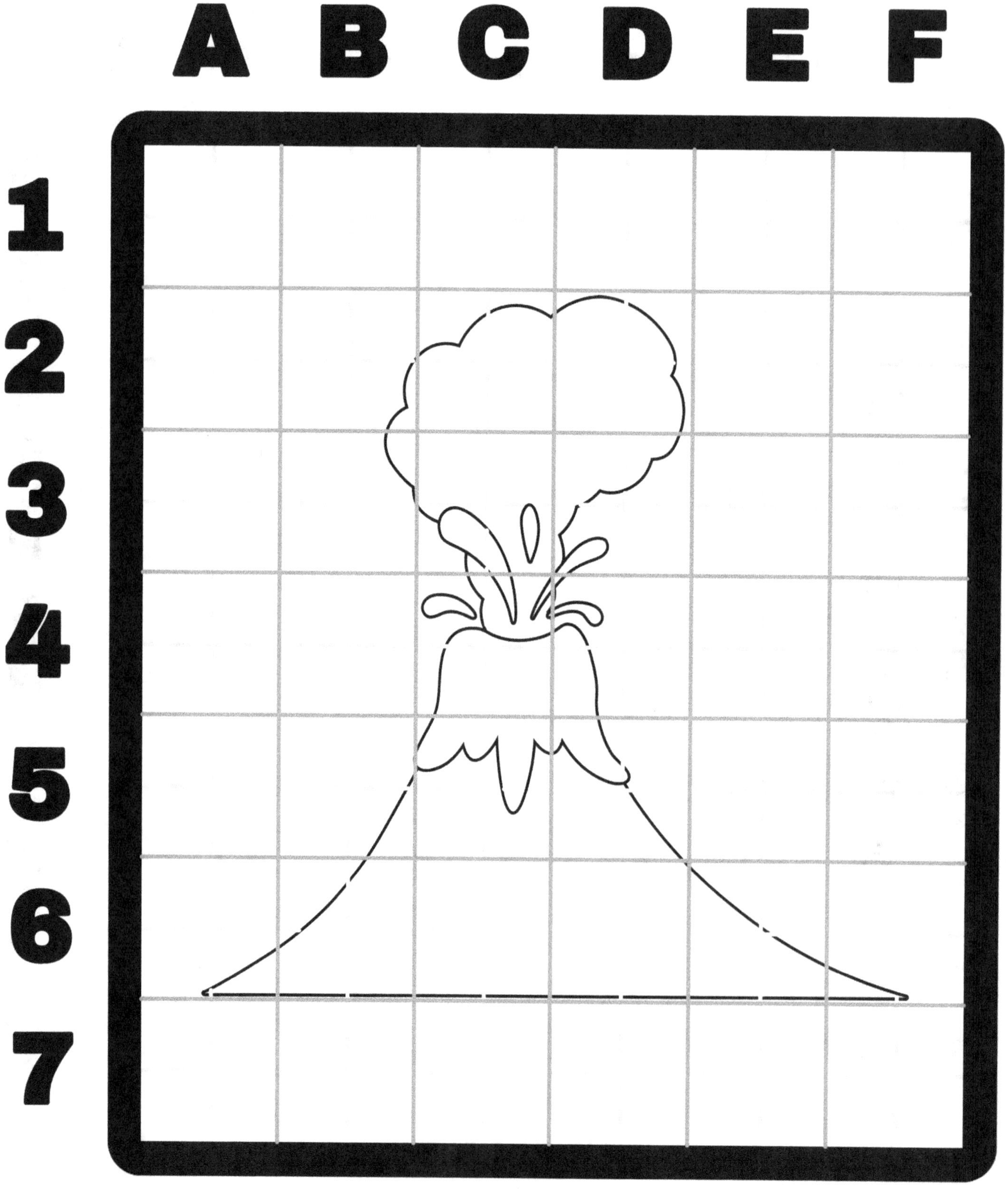
A B C D E F
1
2
3
4
5
6
7

YOUR TURN!

	A	B	C	D	E	F
1						
2						
3						
4						
5						
6						
7						

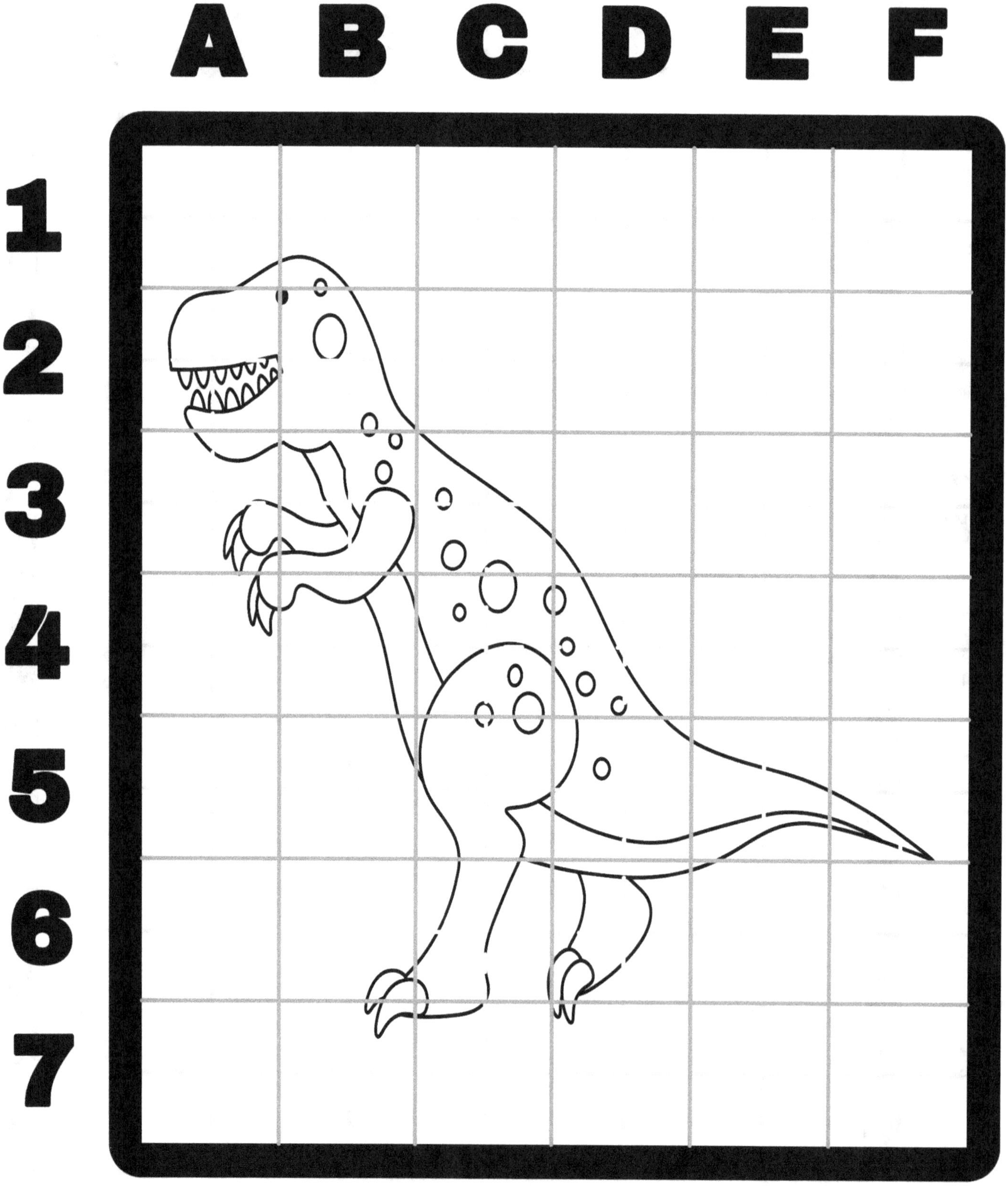
A B C D E F
1
2
3
4
5
6
7

YOUR TURN!

	A	B	C	D	E	F
1						
2						
3						
4						
5						
6						
7						

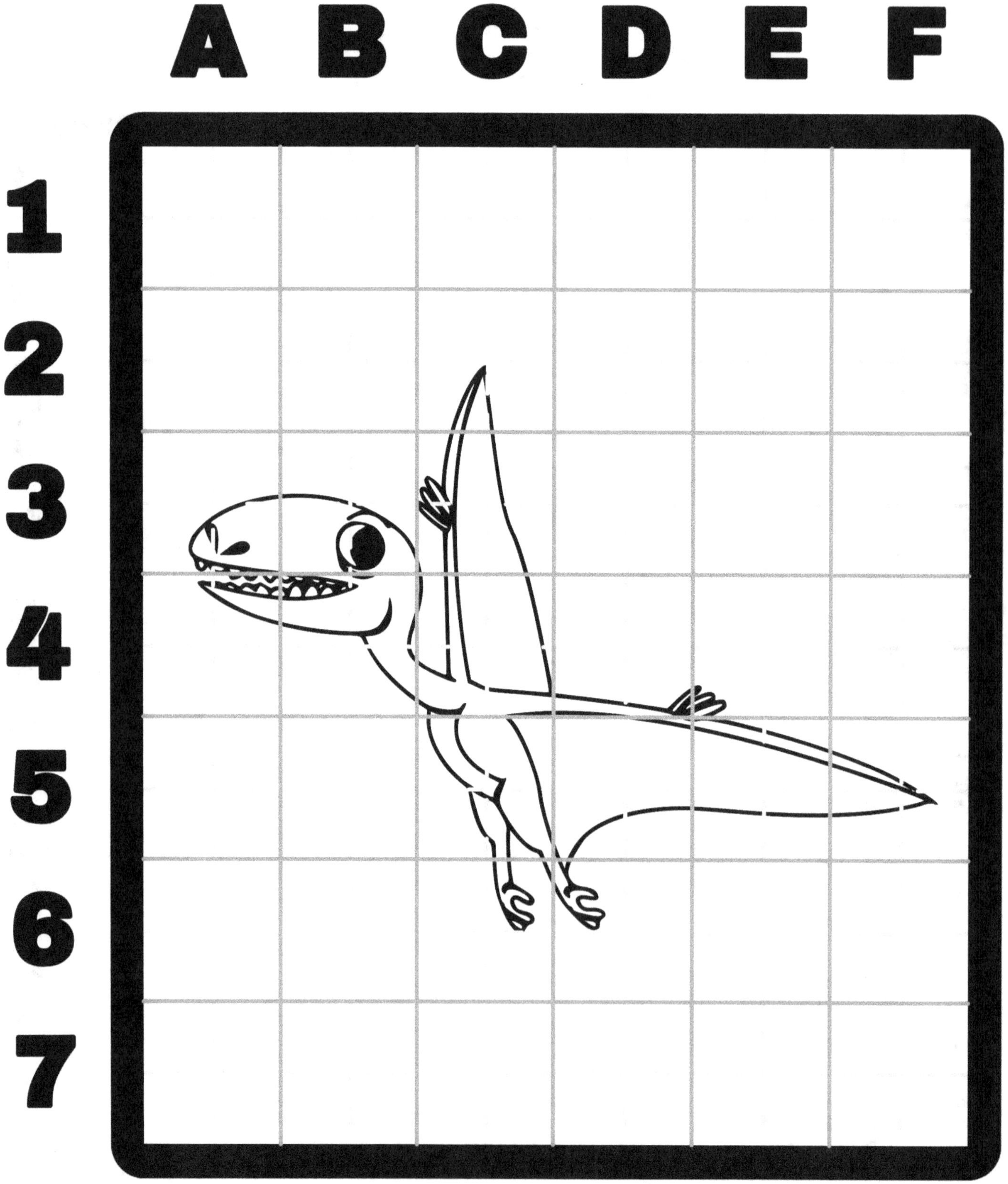
A B C D E F
1
2
3
4
5
6
7

YOUR TURN!

	A	B	C	D	E	F
1						
2						
3						
4						
5						
6						
7						

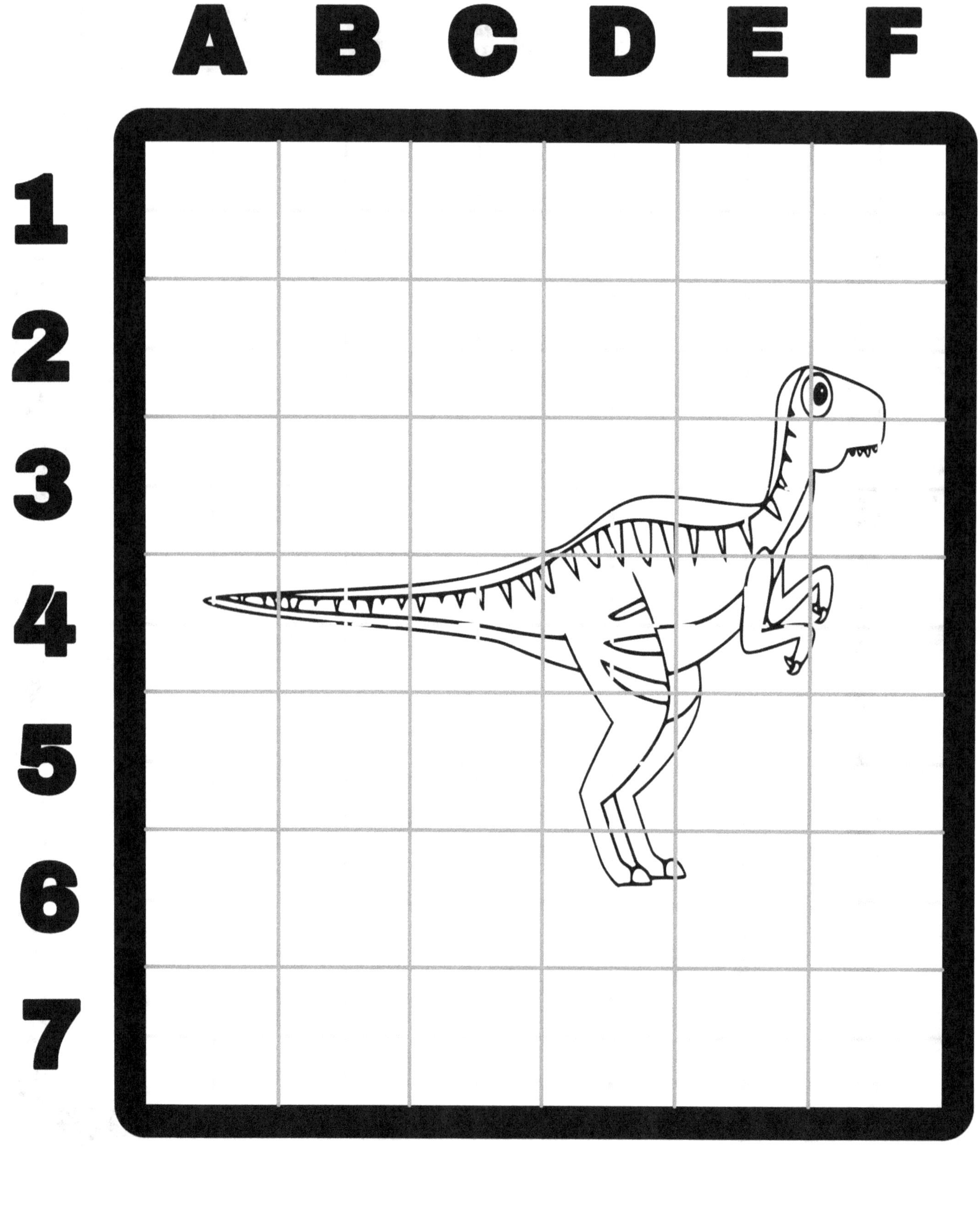
A B C D E F
1
2
3
4
5
6
7

YOUR TURN!

	A	B	C	D	E	F
1						
2						
3						
4						
5						
6						
7						

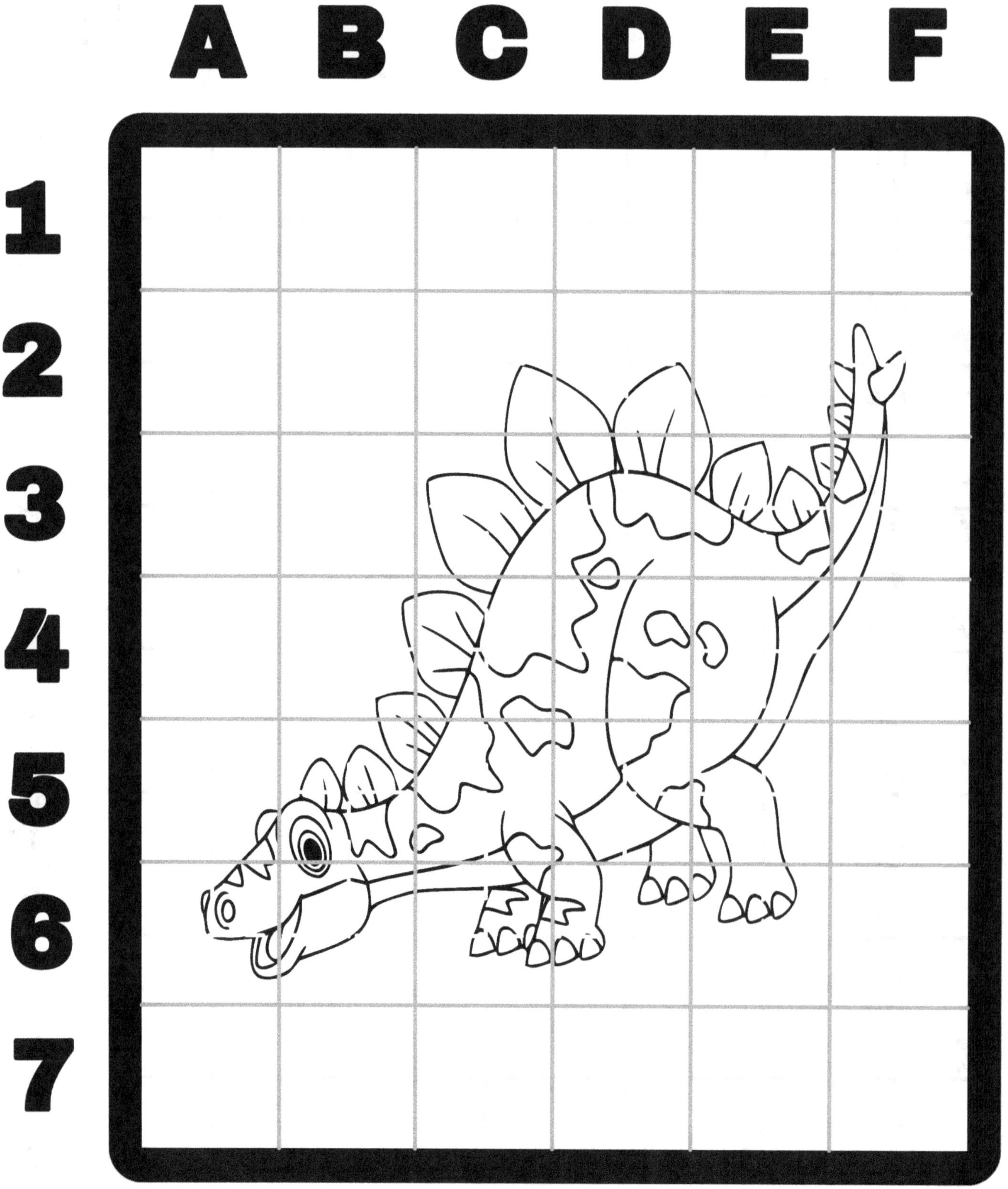
A B C D E F
1
2
3
4
5
6
7

YOUR TURN!

	A	B	C	D	E	F
1						
2						
3						
4						
5						
6						
7						

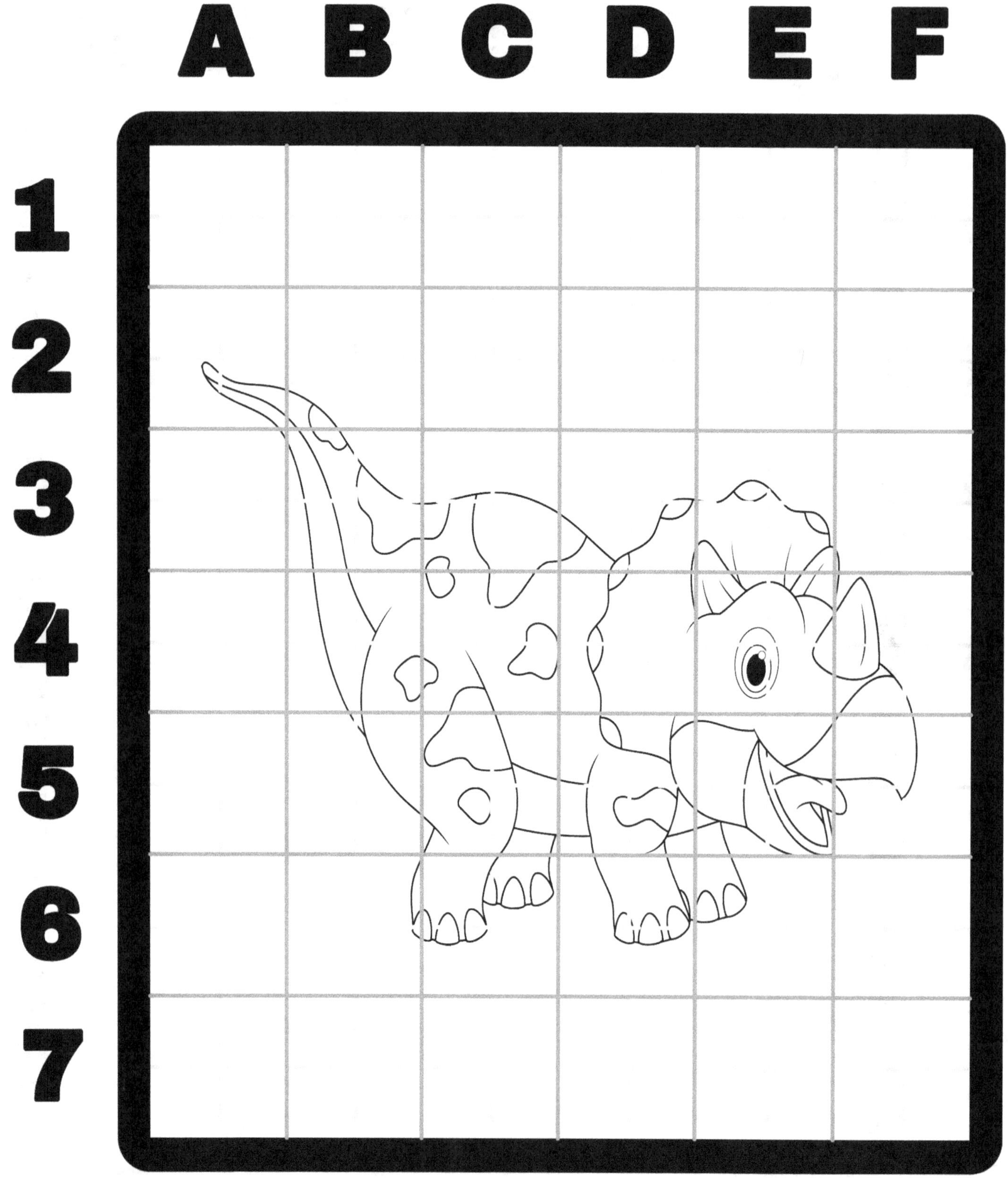
A
B
C
D
E
F
1
2
3
4
5
6
7

YOUR TURN!

	A	B	C	D	E	F
1						
2						
3						
4						
5						
6						
7						

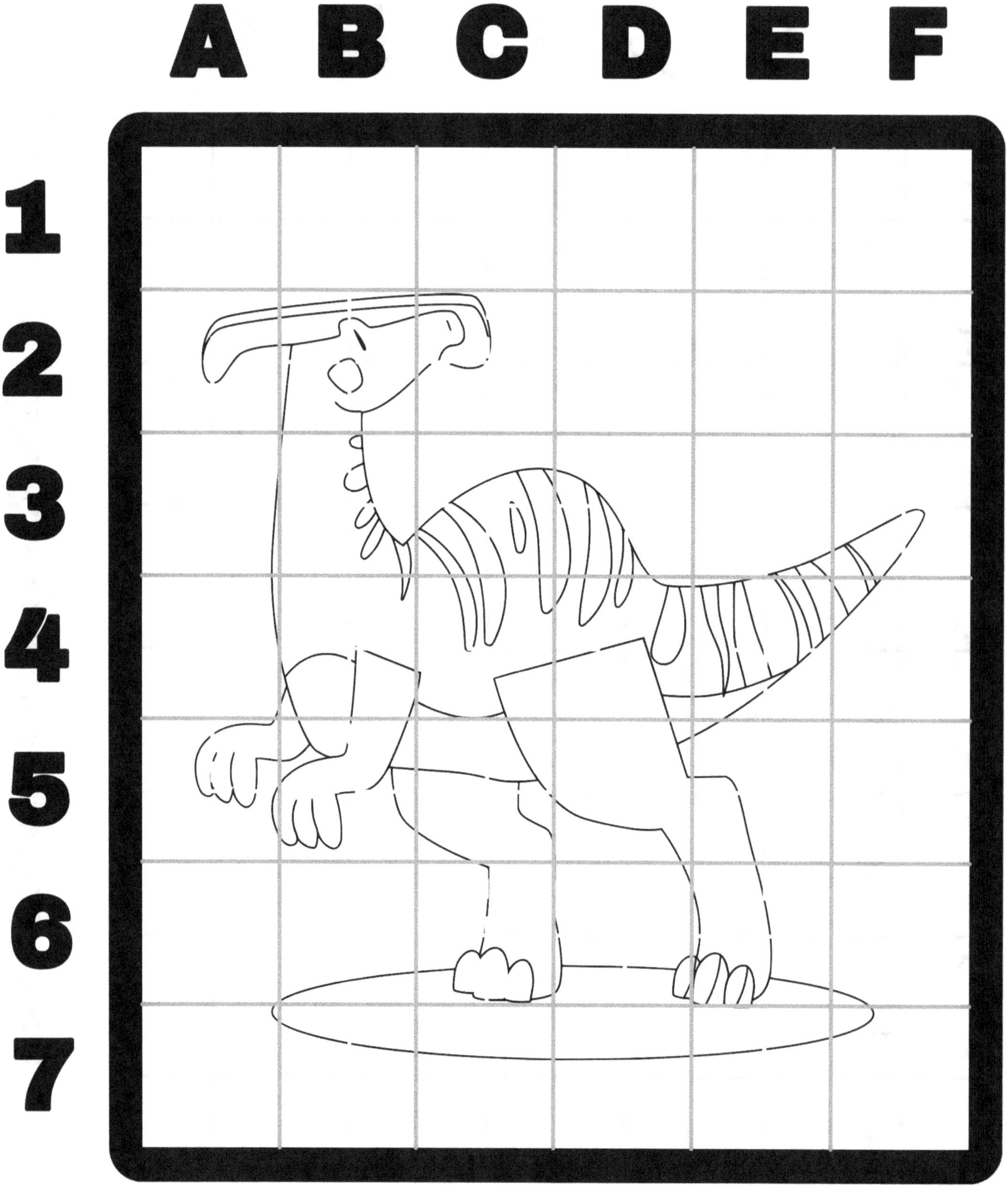
A B C D E F
1
2
3
4
5
6
7

YOUR TURN!

	A	B	C	D	E	F
1						
2						
3						
4						
5						
6						
7						

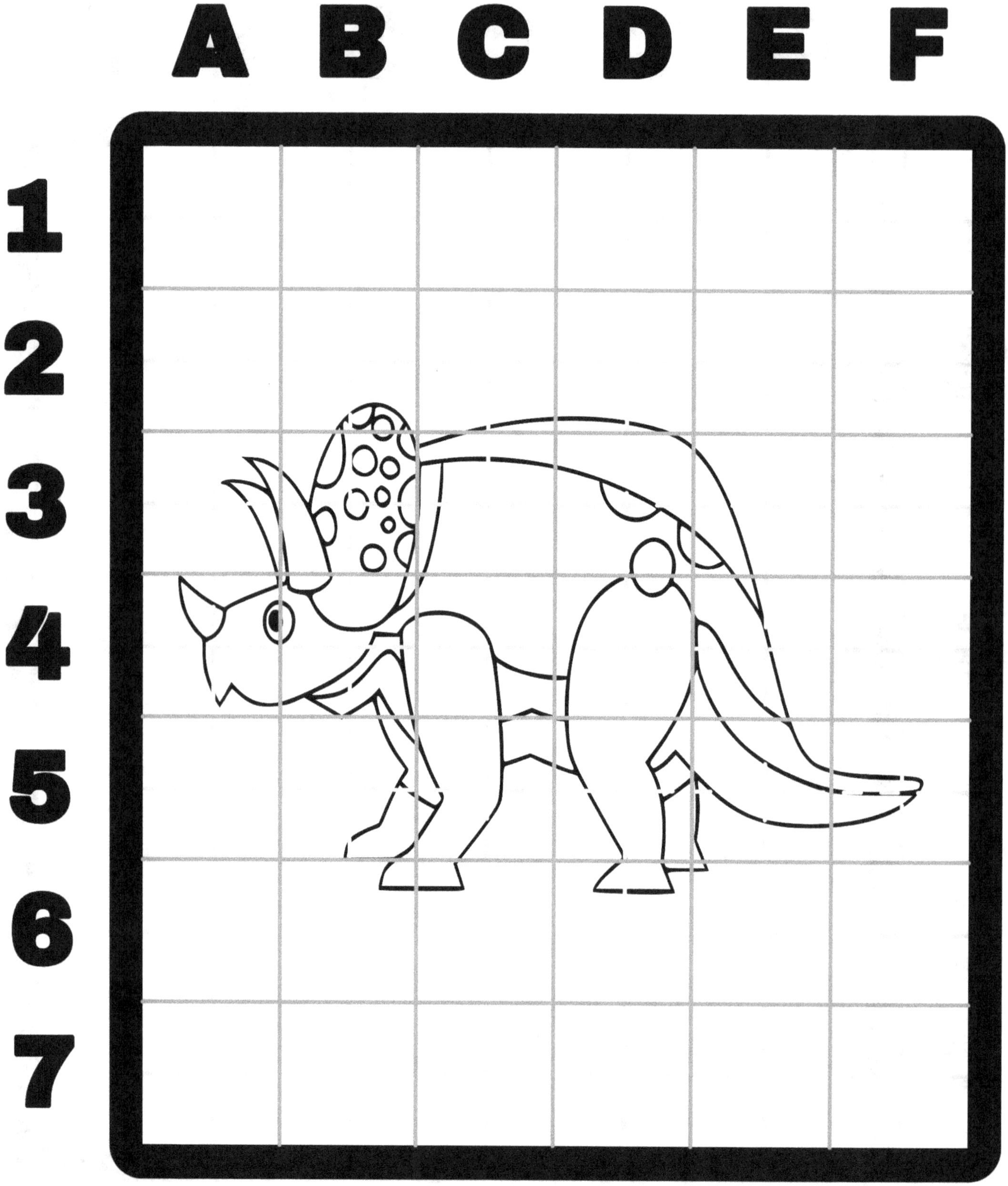
A B C D E F
1
2
3
4
5
6
7

YOUR TURN!

	A	B	C	D	E	F
1						
2						
3						
4						
5						
6						
7						

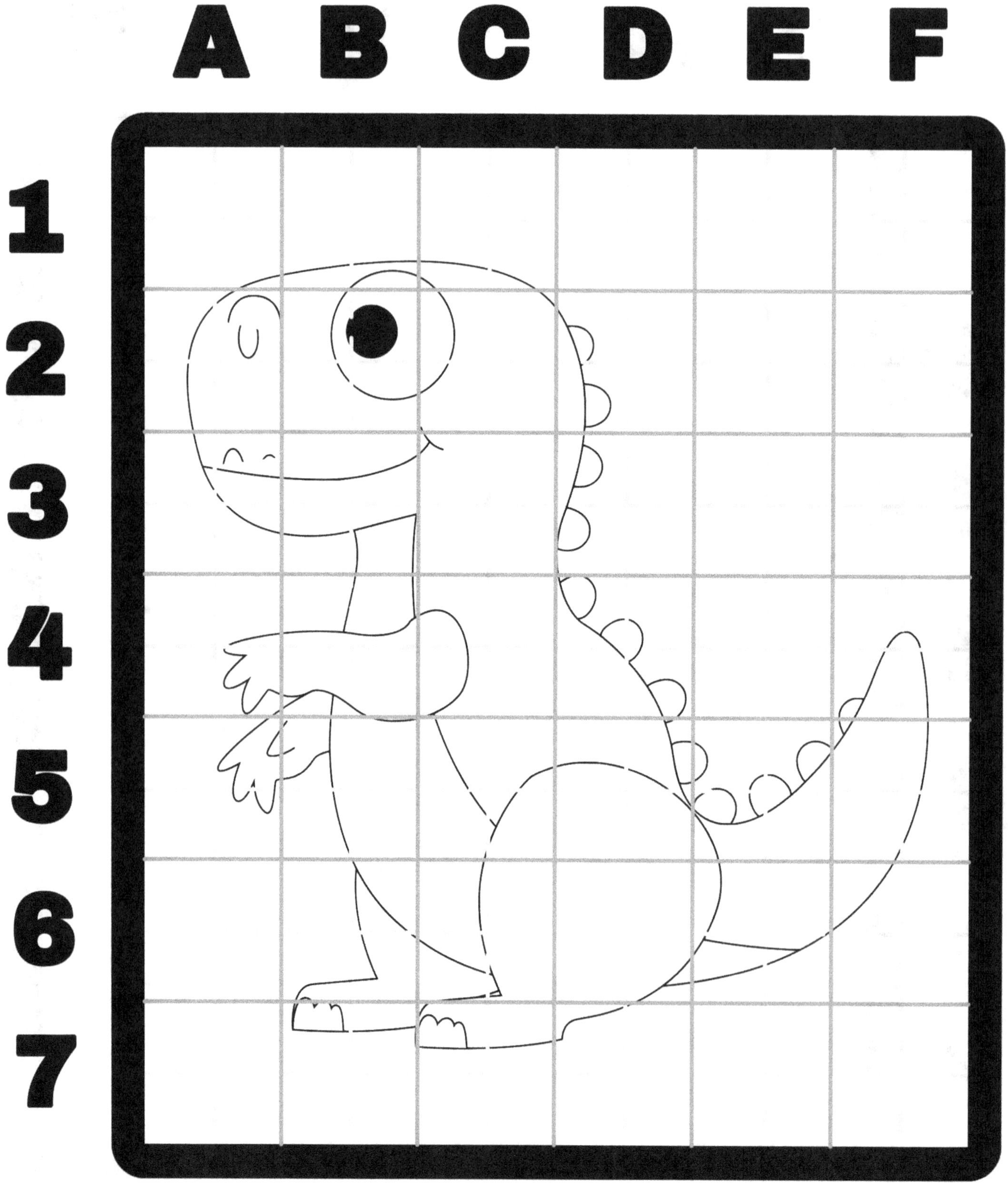
A B C D E F
1
2
3
4
5
6
7

YOUR TURN!

	A	B	C	D	E	F
1						
2						
3						
4						
5						
6						
7						

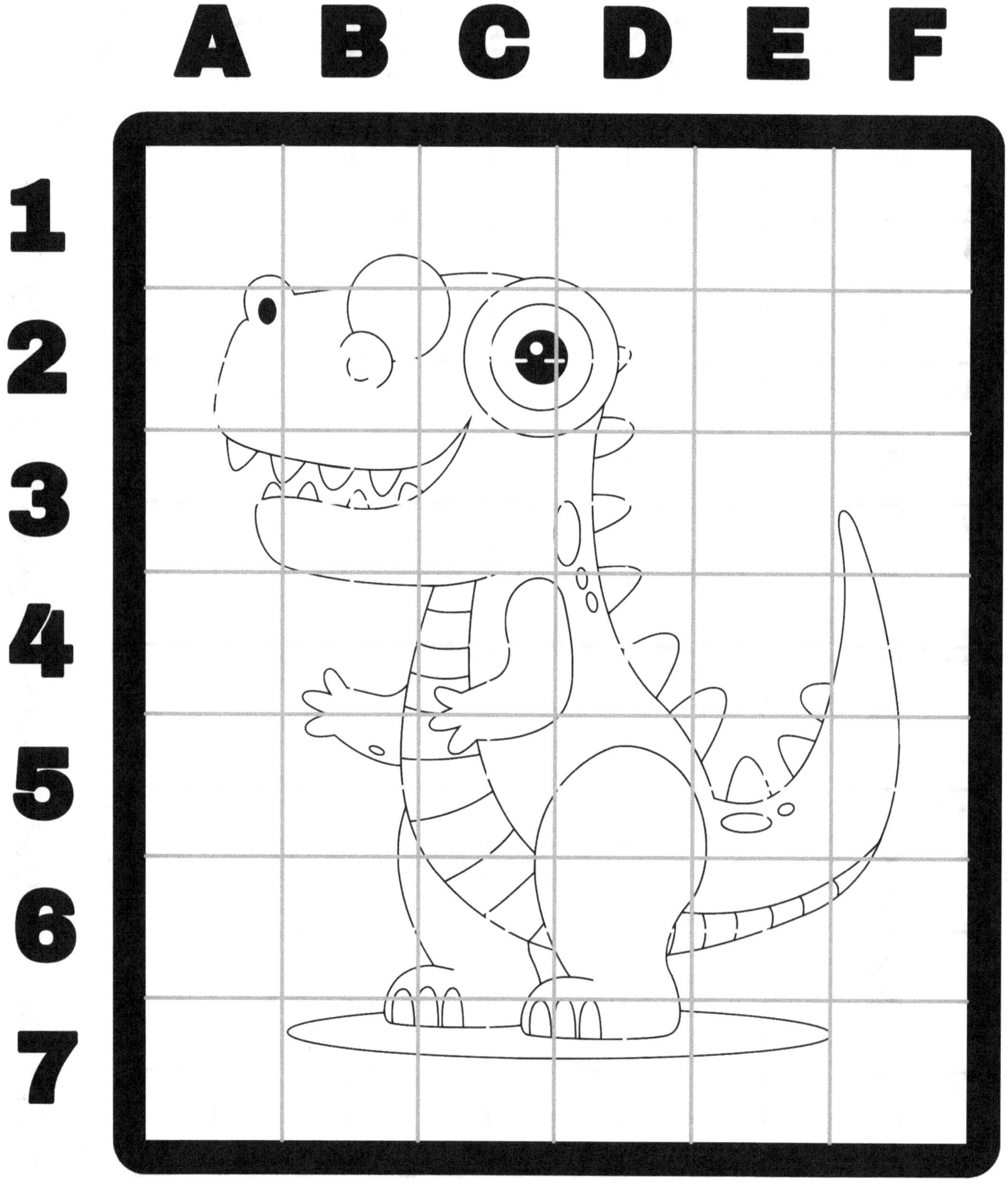
A B C D E F
1
2
3
4
5
6
7

YOUR TURN!

	A	B	C	D	E	F
1						
2						
3						
4						
5						
6						
7						

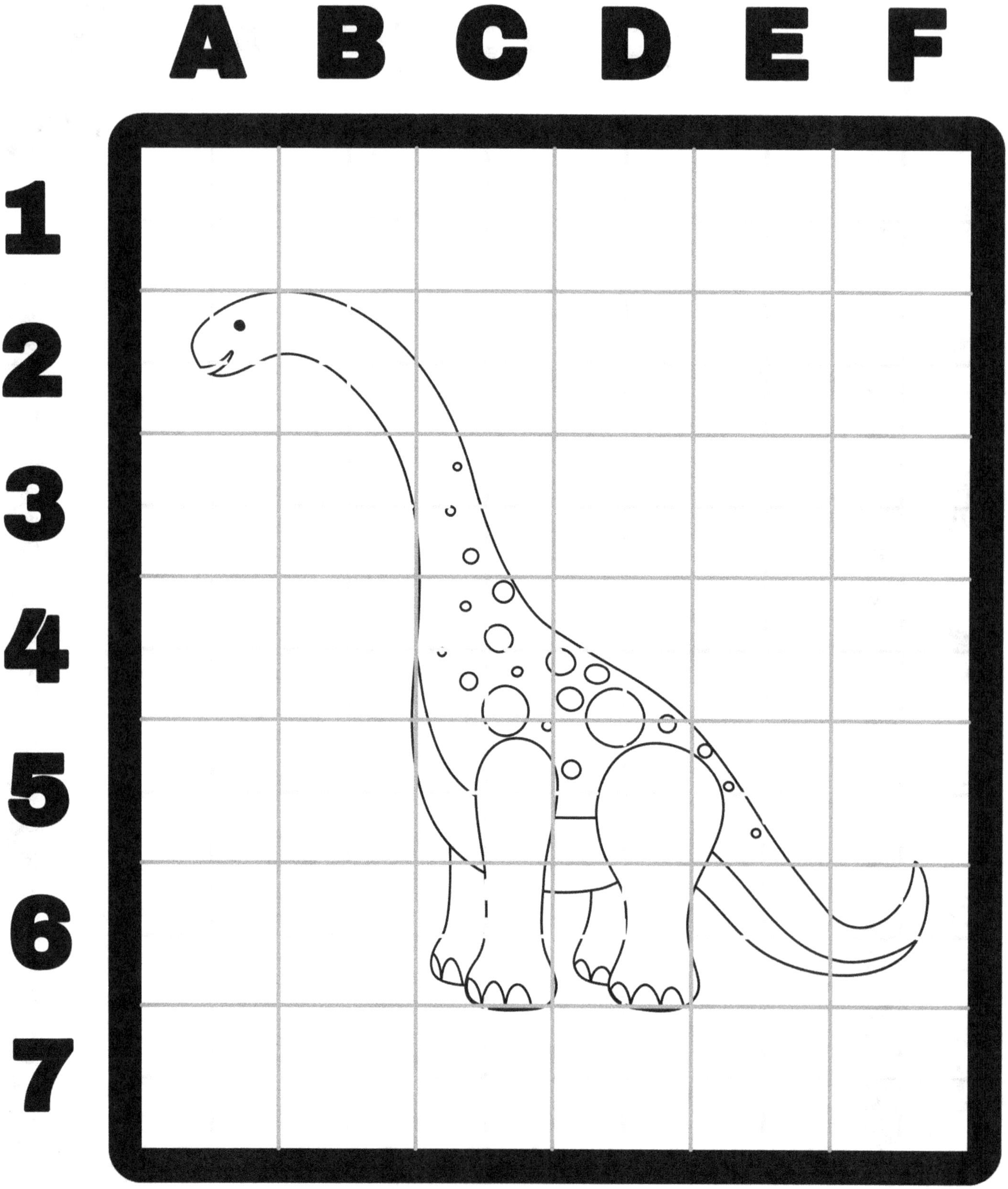
A B C D E F
1
2
3
4
5
6
7

YOUR TURN!

	A	B	C	D	E	F
1						
2						
3						
4						
5						
6						
7						

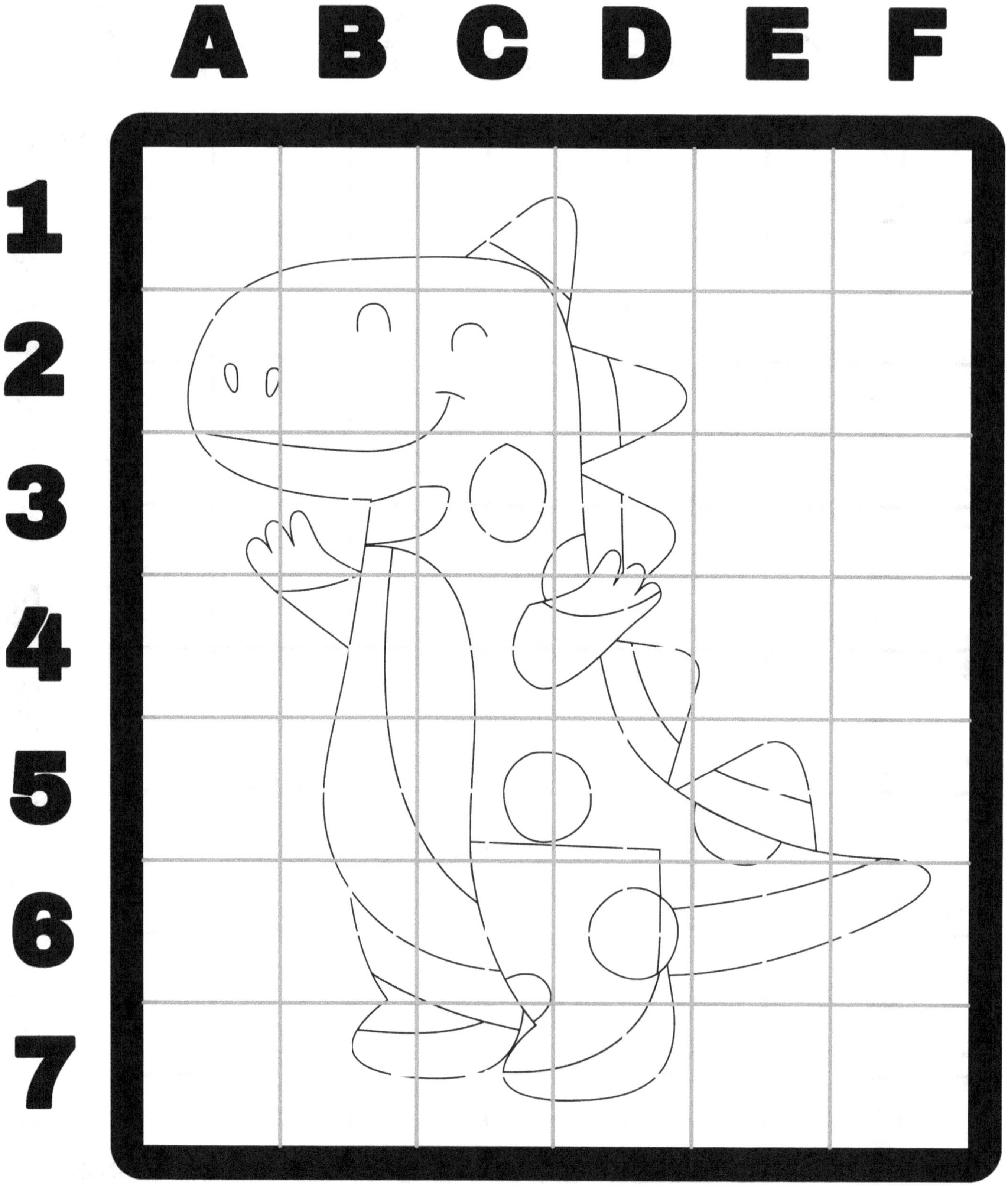
A B C D E F
1
2
3
4
5
6
7

YOUR TURN!

	A	B	C	D	E	F
1						
2						
3						
4						
5						
6						
7						

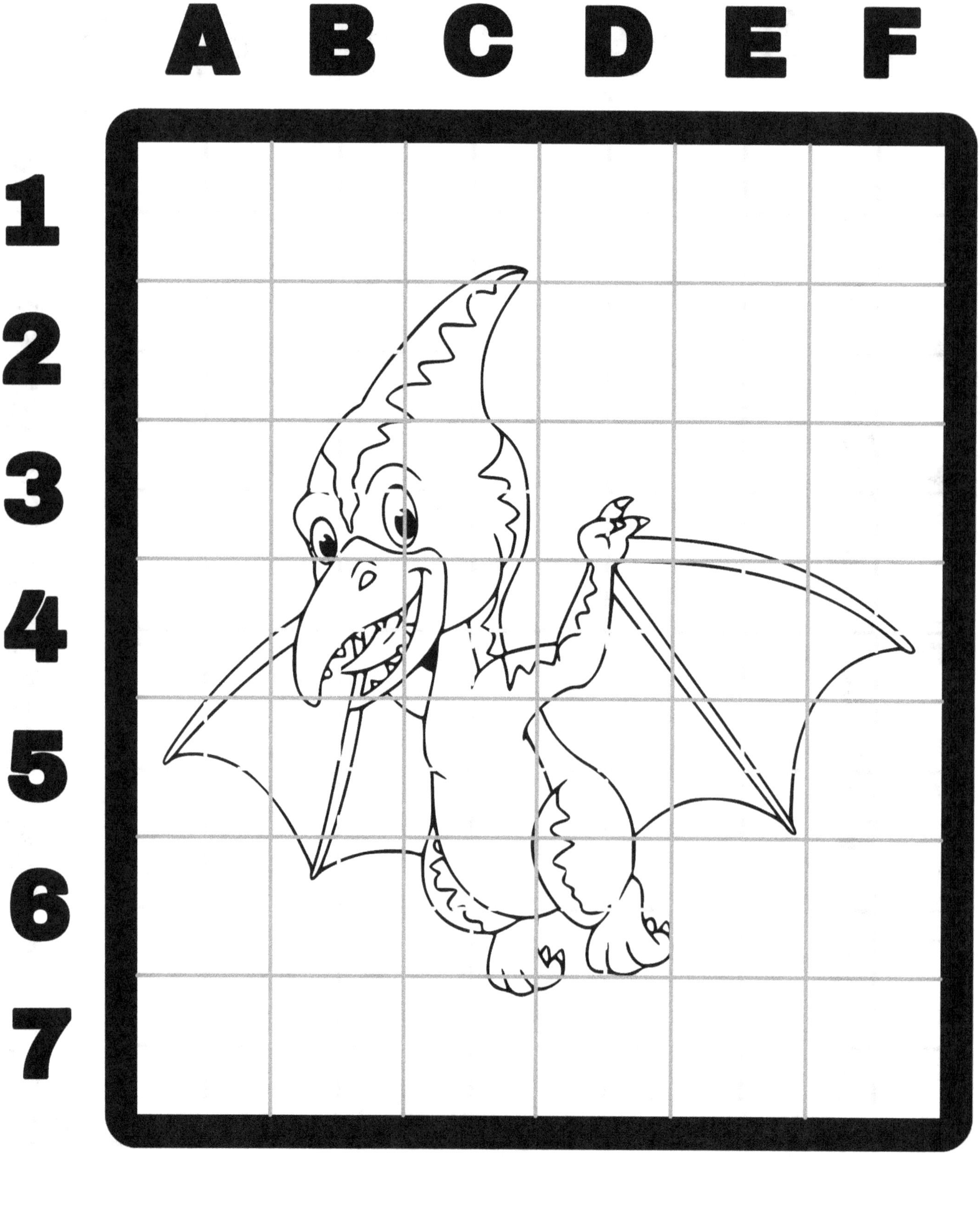
A B C D E F
1
2
3
4
5
6
7

YOUR TURN!

	A	B	C	D	E	F
1						
2						
3						
4						
5						
6						
7						

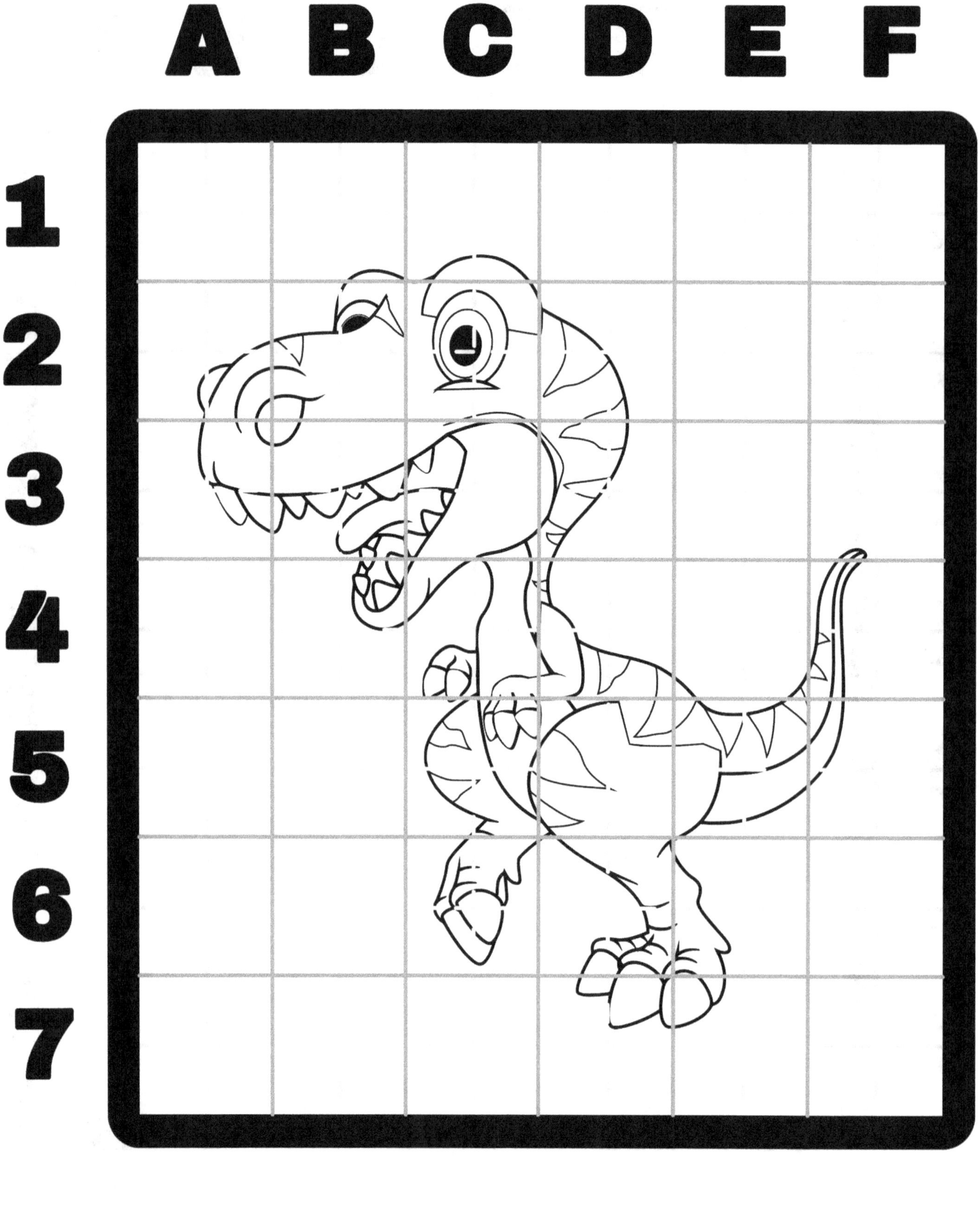
A B C D E F
1
2
3
4
5
6
7

YOUR TURN!

	A	B	C	D	E	F
1						
2						
3						
4						
5						
6						
7						

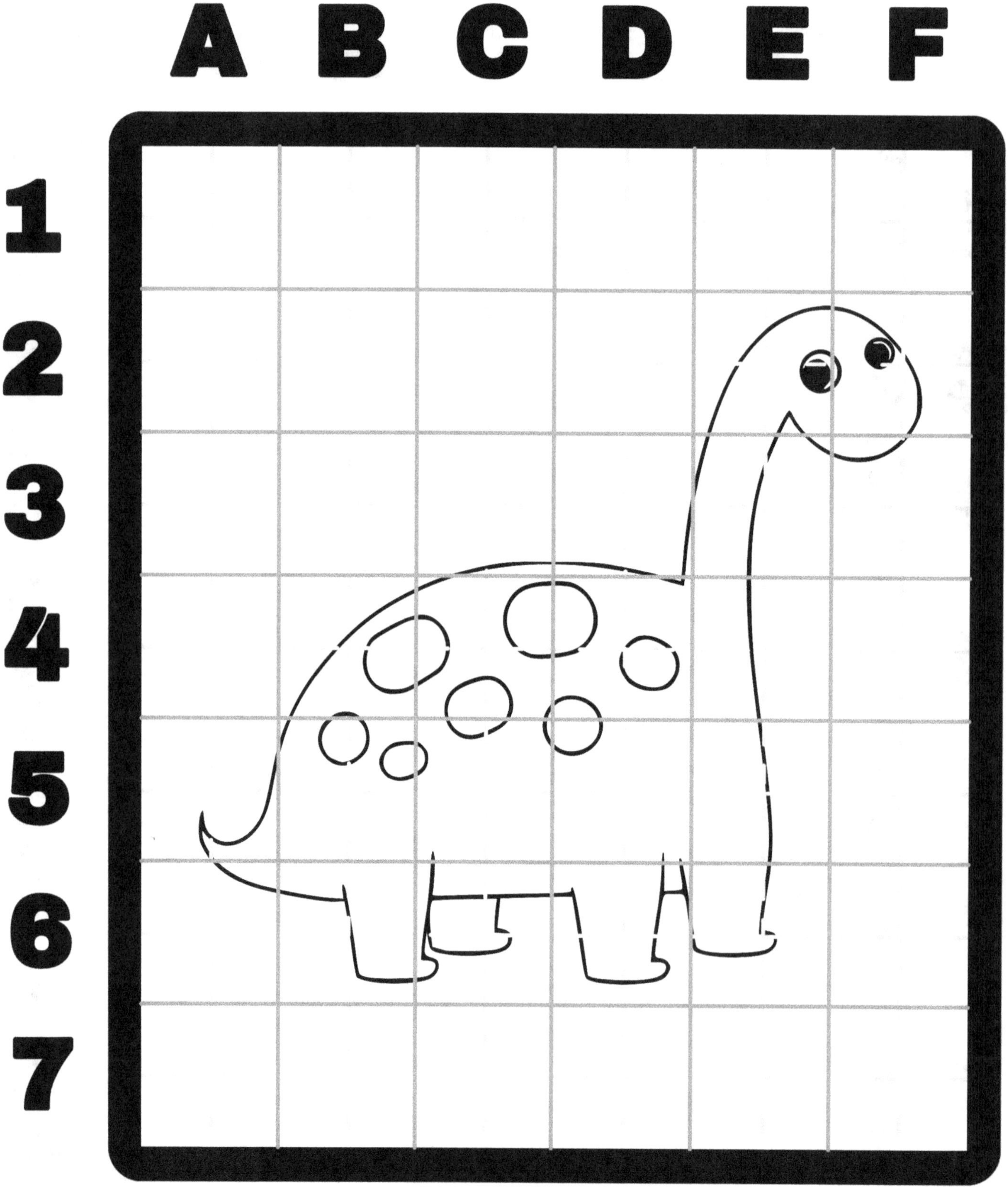
A B C D E F
1
2
3
4
5
6
7

YOUR TURN!

	A	B	C	D	E	F
1						
2						
3						
4						
5						
6						
7						

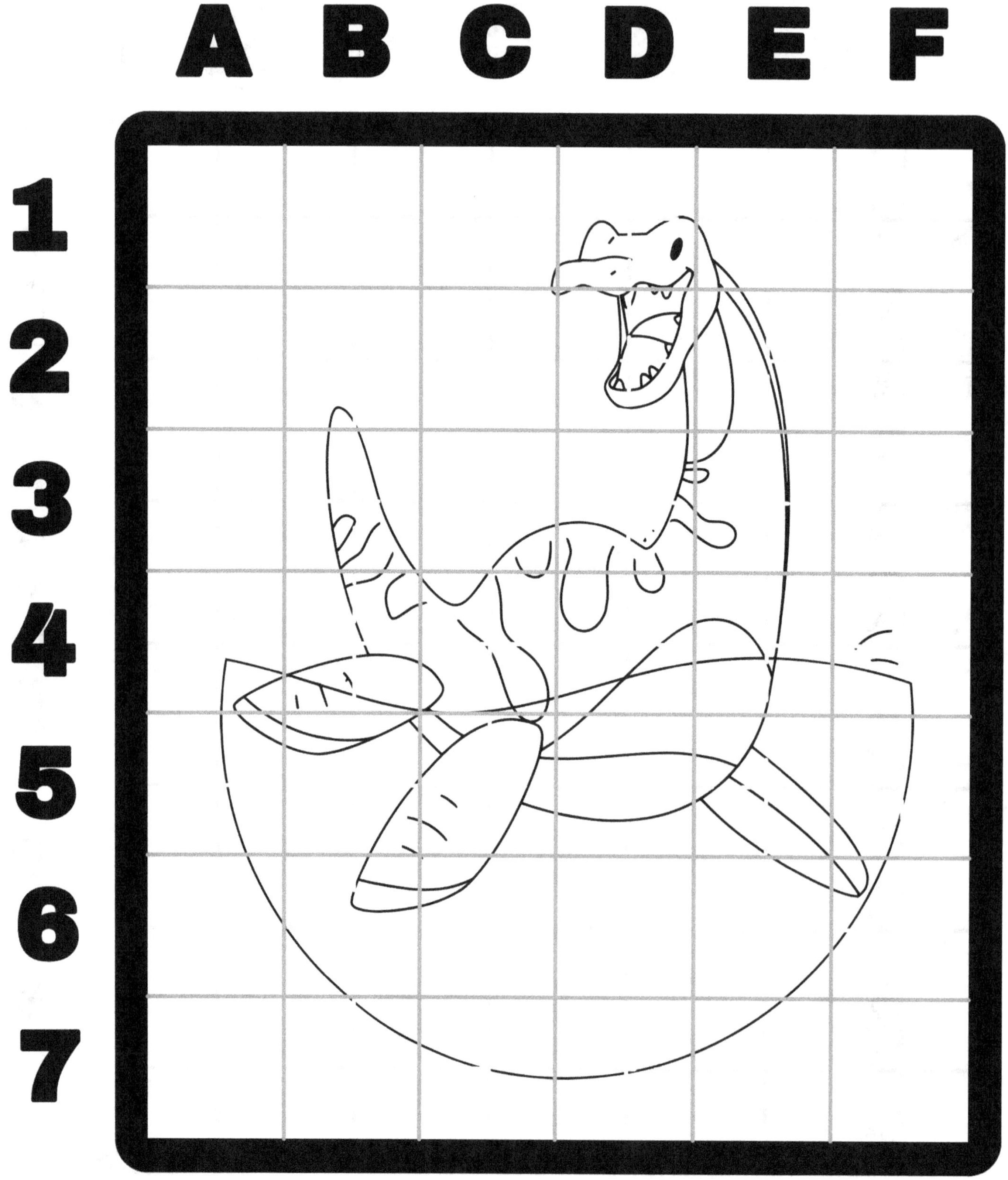
A B C D E F
1
2
3
4
5
6
7

YOUR TURN!

	A	B	C	D	E	F
1						
2						
3						
4						
5						
6						
7						

www.ingramcontent.com/pod-product-compliance
Lightning Source LLC
Chambersburg PA
CBHW080850220526
45467CB00008B/2463